Sioux Arrows
and
Bullets

Also by the author:
Where the Old West Never Died

Sioux Arrows
and
Bullets

by PAUL SANFORD

The Naylor Company
Book Publishers of the Southwest
San Antonio, Texas

Dedication

To my sister, Talva, whose interest in
our family history has provided me with
letters and other important information.

Contents

The Attack on Fort Ridgley

HEADQUARTERS DEPARTMENT OF THE
NORTHWEST[1]
St. Paul, Minn., Sept. 23, 1862

Major General HALLECK,
Washington, D.C.:

You do not seem to be aware of the extent of the Indian outbreaks. The Sioux, 2,600 warriors, are assembled at the Upper Sioux Agency, ready to give battle. . . . All the frontiers of Minnesota to within a short distance of the Mississippi have been depopulated, large towns and villages abandoned and the property and crops of more than 50,000 people totally abandoned.

1

You have no idea of the wide, universal and un-controllable panic everywhere in this country. Over 500 people have been murdered in Minnesota alone and 300 women and children now in captivity. The most horrible massacres have been committed; children nailed alive to trees and houses, women violated and then disemboweled — everything that horrible ingenuity could devise. . . . The troops here are perfectly raw and without discipline.

Jno. Pope, Major General.

There had been a good deal of horseplay among the new recruits on the long march to Mankato, where we'd gone to be mustered in. Now on August 19, 1862, four days later, we were slogging along the muddy trail to Fort Ridgley in a darkly sober mood. We'd been in a hurry to get to the fort, but apprehensive about what we'd find when we arrived. As we climbed over the last low ridge and saw the flag flying above the parade ground I felt my heart lift.

Sergeant Frank Pierce waved a hand at it and voiced my own thoughts, "Well, that's a relief," he grinned. "I've been repeating a small prayer that we'd get there before the Indians did. From the bloody disaster that courier was yelling at us at Schwartz' I wouldn't have been surprised to find the fort surrounded — or maybe captured and burned."

More than a hundred of us from Freeborn and Faribault counties had enlisted in the Ninth Regiment Minnesota Volunteers, under Captain Pettit, expecting to join General Grant's army. Instead, we'd been urgently ordered to come north to fight against the Indian uprising along the Minnesota River. We'd been told we'd be issued rifles and uniforms at Mankato. That had been our first foul-up. There were neither rifles nor any supplies for us. Instead, we'd had to disperse among various abandoned farms and cut grain for food for our whole company while Captain Pettit rode to Fort Snelling near St. Paul to unravel the red tape.

2

It had been a worrisome four days. Rumors were coming down from settlers along the upper river that Indians were stealing every horse they could find. Women and children were leaving both the Upper Sioux Agency at Yellow Medicine and the Lower Agency near Redwood Falls. Settlers near where we were working scoffed at the rumors. We didn't know what to believe. Sergeant Pierce and I had kept Platoons Two and Four together all we could, for the safety of numbers, but as Corporal Cook said, "I feel plumb naked without a gun. If the Indians attacked we couldn't even defend ourselves, let alone help any settlers."

But when the courier, on a lathered mule, had stopped at a cluster of cabins near where we'd been cutting wheat and digging potatoes, Pierce and I had hurried over to Jud Schwartz' cabin to get the news. The rider galloped on as we got there.[2]

"The Reservation Indians are on the rampage," Jud told us. "The Lower Agency is burning and a whole mess of soldiers and settlers have been killed. We're heading for Fort Ridgley. That's closer than New Ulm. Besides, New Ulm may be under attack. There's nothing safe west of the river. That rider is going to Mankato and St. Peter to try to get help."

"We'd come with you, if we had enough guns to help," I said. "There are only six rifles and two revolvers among the whole fifty of us. You might attract less attention alone."

"Better come anyway. They must have muskets at the fort. They need men. That rider said Lieutenant Gere has less than thirty men on their feet. Your bunch of men might scare any Indians we meet into leaving us alone."

"Maybe you're right. We'll load up a wagon with potatoes and what wheat we've flailed out and come along."

Four families of settlers in three wagons and our fifty men marching behind the wagon of supplies must have

3

looked impressive. I had the feeling that there were Indians about. My heart choked up into my throat as we topped every ridge, but we were lucky. Jud Schwartz knew the trails, even if he'd never fired a rifle, and he led us to the fort along the winding roads leading there from the southeast.

The fort was already swarming with people when we hiked in. Pierce and I searched out the Commanding Officer, Lieutenant Gere, and reported our men.

"Sergeants Frank Pierce and Allen Morgan, sir, Company B, Ninth Regiment Minnesota Volunteers, reporting for any duty you can give us. We can fight and our men have had some drill and will obey orders, but we haven't been issued any rifles. Can you supply us guns?"

"What, no muskets at all? That is bad. I need fighters. We have a few extra Springfields I can pass out to settlers who seem to know which end to shoot with, and you can use all I have left. Looks like you need uniforms, too. Where is your commanding officer?"

"Captain Pettit had to go to Fort Snelling to get new orders. We'd been ordered to hurry to Mankato to be sworn into the army, but the Commissary Sergeant on the supply boat that met us there had no authority to issue supplies until we were in. We've been digging potatoes and cutting wheat on the abandoned farms while we waited. We brought about twenty sacks of potatoes and thirty bushels of new wheat. Can you use it?"

"I should say we can! Over three hundred settlers have taken shelter here last night and today. I'm trying to house them in the stables and those old barracks yonder. The rest of them are camping out in sheds as best they can. Find some place for your men to sleep out of the rain tonight. Be careful with cooking fires. Bring your extra food over to the commissary and about thirty of your best riflemen over to the barracks; that's all the muskets I have left.

"I'm only in temporary command here. Captain Marsh was in command until he was ambushed yesterday at Red-

4

wood Ferry and lost most of his forty-eight-man detail. I
sent another courier last night to my senior officer, Lieutenant Sheehan, Company C, Fifth Regiment Minnesota
Volunteers. He should be on the way down from Fort
Ripley. Pray God he gets here soon. I look for an attack
almost any time. It'll soon be dark but we're raising barricades between the log buildings. I'd like to have your
men help with that. Most of my men are out on picket
duty, watching for Indians. My Company B was the one
ambushed at Redwood Ferry," he ended grimly. I felt
sorry for the youngster. He was bearing up under a hard
and sudden load with a man's determination, for all he
was only nineteen.

"There may be more of our Ninth Regiment coming
in, sir," Sergeant Pierce said. "Two more platoons under
Sergeants Del Tinney and John Calvin are working west
of the Minnesota River under Lieutenant Shaw. We sent
a messenger to find them after the rider came through to
warn the settlers."

"Good! We'll need every man we can get. I see
that a few of you have rifles. That looks like one of the
new Henrys."

"Yes, sir. I brought my Henry .44. Sergeant Pierce has
his own .45 Sharps and four men have squirrel rifles. Two
of the others have revolvers. We were glad to have even
that much for defense, when we found out what a hornet's
nest we'd gotten into. All that the settlers who came with us
could produce were two old fowling pieces."

"Can any of you make bread or bannock?" Lieutenant
Gere wanted to know. "We're almost out of hard bread."

"This new wheat is too soft for making bread, sir. We've
been boiling up some wheat every night for mush in the
morning. We've had to live on boiled wheat and potatoes
except for one hog we butchered. Indians stole most of the
cattle and horses down along the river, but they missed the
pig. We left a receipt, signed by our Lieutenant Hollister,
for anything we used from any of the farms. Our men didn't

5

want to hike back home to Freeborn after coming all that way up to Mankato. And the merchants there were urging everyone available to help with the harvest. They're short of flour at Mankato, since their mill burned."

"Well, I'm glad you came here. Sergeant Jones needs all the help he can get on those barricades."

We pitched in with building barricades between the commissary and the officers quarters strung out toward the stables. I listened to a lot of rumors being discussed by the settlers who were helping with the work. The knowing ones, who had been at the fort all day, claimed that Captain Marsh's men had been ambushed at Redwood Ferry while they were trying to protect the settlers, and most of the detail had been killed in the first volley of firing. The ferry was about ten miles up the river from Fort Ridgley. The soldiers never got as far as the Lower Agency. The atrocities reported by the settlers were unbelievable. Some of them were still too frightened to tell what they had seen. I went over and asked Sergeant Pierce what he thought about it all.

"It all boils down to one thing," he decided. "Fort Ridgley is sure to be attacked soon. And I expect there will be all of the four hundred Indians they say laid the ambush up at Redwood Ferry. Let's get on with these barricades."

We detailed two men to find a shed for our blankets and supplies, and to build a fire for boiling potatoes and wheat and the last of our pork. We'd need as good a supper as we could provide for the men. Cutting and flailing wheat had started soon after daylight; we'd walked nearly ten miles to the fort, and still had time for several hours on the barricades.

Lieutenant Gere came over about dark, to where Frank and I were helping our men to place a tree trunk between the stables and a smaller building to the northeast. Some of our men were just coming in from the woods to the southwest, where they'd been cutting trees, while men with horses had been snaking the logs up to us for extending the barricades. It was too dark for working in the woods, but we

6

were using the last light for extending our circle of protection.

"You were right when you said your men could work," the Lieutenant said with approval. "Send a couple of your men over to the commissary for a leg of beef. You're entitled to it after all the work you've done — not to mention the wheat and potatoes you brought in. I'll talk with Lieutenant Sheehan as soon as he arrives, and see if we can't muster you in as an emergency measure, and issue you blankets and supplies. Your men obey orders like they've had good training. That's more than I can say about most of the settlers. And some of them are even demanding special protection and an escort to Fort Snelling. That's impossible!"[3]

"They must be crazy!" I exploded. "I can see we aren't very well fortified, sir, but they'd never have a chance to cross the prairies and woods. Can't they understand that there's no transportation available for their children, or food?"

"Only a few of them have been unreasonable. They are just frightened. Now that they've lost their homes, they're also angry. Others have taken the trouble more calmly and are trying to be helpful. The ones who were hurt the worst seem to be most helpful in getting others settled in the barracks and behind the log walls. They've brought in the injured and fed the children. Many of the women have lost their menfolk. Some of them have babies to look after. We have to defend them."

"We'll help. That's what we enlisted for. All of us who can get guns will help fight."

"Well, we'll see what tomorrow brings. Pick out a good leg of beef, Sergeant, and give the men a good supper."

"Thanks a lot, Lieutenant." I had to admire the young fellow's spunk. He was doing the best he could with a tough responsibility, and some of the settlers I'd seen were ignorant and bull-headed. Many of them could barely understand English.

"Fortunately, we corralled some of the cattle before the Indians ran off all the stock that was out grazing," he told

7

us. "We have enough beef for several days. I sent out scouts to locate the Indians. I hope they'll get back soon. In any case, we'll double the pickets tonight. The Indian Agent told me that the Sioux are afraid to fight at night, but I'm taking no chances. We'll expect a fight any minute."

"How many Indians have gone on a rampage?"

"Sergeant Bishop told me there were three or four hundred warriors who attacked them at Redwood Ferry. But he may have been excited and overestimated."

I hoped that Sergeant Bishop had very greatly over-estimated. Like some of the others, I was a little nervous at the idea of fighting Indians — when the odds were five to one. Only a few of us had ever been under fire. Both Frank Pierce and I had been in the Battle of Bull Run the year before, in July, 1861, where we'd both been wounded, and later discharged to recover from the wounds. That's why we'd been elected as sergeants at the same time Schoolmaster Pettit had been elected as captain. We'd known how to drill the men. We'd put our platoons through maneuvers evenings and Sundays all summer.

As we walked over to where our men were eating supper, Frank called my attention to the fieldpieces in the artillery park by the commissary building. I'd already noticed them, two six-pounders, three howitzers, a twelve-pounder, and a big twenty-four-pounder under waterproof covers, each with its proper caisson, also waterproofed.

"They may not have rifles for us but I'll bet they'll be glad to find out you were in the artillery at Manassas. I have a hunch we're going to need good artillery to protect these barricades if the savages attack in numbers," Frank told me.

"I'll be glad to help with a fieldpiece, but I'd hate to try to fend off four hundred savages with no more defense than we have here." Frank nodded agreement.

There was one bit of news to brighten the early morning conversation around the cooking fires on Wednesday, August 20. About dawn, a tall officer they greeted as Lieutenant Sheehan rode in with a squad of forty-six men. With them were a young lieutenant and a gray-haired sergeant. They

8

said that they had ridden nearly one hundred and fifty miles from Fort Ripley, in less than thirty hours. They'd made the last forty-four miles from Glencoe in nine and a half hours, mostly in darkness. They were swaying on their feet, but I saw the same look of pleased relief on Sheehan's face that I'd seen on Frank's when we had seen the flag flying over the fort.

The confidence of the garrison lifted visibly at once. Sheehan and his men were too busy to be interrupted, so Frank and I again put our men to work on improving the defenses.

Scouts returned from the area near the Minnesota River, and the rumor spread that they'd seen several hundred lodges. I hoped the report was an exaggeration, but later that day, when the Indians came riding in from the west on their piebald ponies, they seemed to cover the whole prairie west of the fort.

Sergeant Pierce had been working beside me. We'd stopped to rest for a moment, after lifting another log onto the barricade. He was admiring the fieldpieces when one of the outer pickets came running in to yell, "Indians!" He didn't need to yell. We could see them. It looked like everyone in the fort had run out to watch.

Suddenly Frank said, "Where are all the warriors? That crowd is all women and old men. I'll bet the savages are down in the ravines, creeping up on us."

If he was right, we didn't have much chance of defending ourselves and getting out of there alive. Once we let the Indians break our lines and get in to hand-to-hand fighting, we'd be licked. They'd be hacking and knifing us. We'd be shooting more of our own people than Indians.

Fort Ridgley wasn't, in any sense, a fortified place. It had no wall and the buildings were scattered in a rough diamond shape, with two stone buildings on the north and west points, and with officers' quarters on the southwest and near the stables and sutler's warehouse. There was a row of log barracks on the north. A string of log and pole sheds

9

were east and north of the stables, and the big, bare drill ground lay in the middle.

All of the fieldpieces composing the artillery park beside the stone commissary were in place, facing out toward the open, where the Indians had appeared, but not where they could be a defense against a charge from the ravines to the south and southwest. Another big ravine to the northeast came within a hundred yards of the sheds in that direction. Sheds could certainly make a shelter for any Indians slipping in from that ravine. Fear gripped like an angry hand on my heart, as the long roll sounded assembly for the garrison.

I yelled back at Frank, "Let's get our rifles — and on the double."

By the time we'd run across the parade ground to our camp, we heard the pickets firing out beyond the shed to the northeast. Soon guns were booming and barking on all sides of us except to the west. A bugle sounded as men were still running in from digging entrenchments near the stable. They were lining up in front of the barracks as Lieutenant Sheehan ran out. He had been awakened by the first roll of the drum, and began calling off stations to the sergeants, even while they were mustering their men. I soon learned that he'd had experience with the Indians all summer, when his Company C had helped with the distribution of the annuity beef to the Indians at Yellow Medicine in June and July. Now his orders came clear and rapid. Squads were running out to the farther buildings as fast as they could go. Single pickets were racing back toward us, away from the ravines. It was all confusing to me but probably purposeful to Sheehan.

Sergeant Jones, in red striped artillery trousers and with red tabs on his blouse, was directing a squad in hauling a six-pounder around the barracks, toward the gap between the officers' quarters and the stone buildings. A lieutenant was bawling orders to another squad hauling a howitzer to the north of the log barracks, where it could sweep the whole area on the north and over to the northeast.

I noticed some of my men looking like they wondered

10

what to do, so I called out, "Give 'em a shoulder with that gun, boys," and it was soon rolling at a run. Others tailed onto the caisson and had it rolling too. As it bounced, I murmured a prayerful hope that the shells and powder in it were well packed and padded. Another gun went bouncing out to the sheds to the northeast. A score of our men with muskets, formed into a nicely drilled unit beside it. Corporal Cook was following my hurried orders with skill and decision.

By that time, there were regular soldiers lining the strung-out buildings all around the parade ground. It was empty, except for the women and children of the settlers and some of their menfolk who kept urging them to get inside the stone barracks and log buildings. Over all the noise, I could hear the whooping of savages gathering at the edge of the gully to the northeast.

Frank Pierce came trotting over to where some of our boys were helping with the howitzer northwest of the barracks, just as Lieutenant Sheehan called to us. He appeared to be perfectly calm, in spite of all the commotion he'd started and all the horrors of a massacre if his orders weren't effective in stopping the savages.

"I've got a job for several of your men," he said. "Get them together, and some of you bring those teams tied to the corral. Our ammunition for the spare fieldpieces is stored in that wooden magazine out there in the open to the northwest. Take both wagons and bring back everything in it. Any Indians who try to attack you will have to cross the open prairie for a long way. Sergeant Bishop's men will give you cover."

"Yes, sir."

"Take all that spare ammunition down to the bakery building. Be careful how you handle it. But hurry!"

Sergeant Pierce's bull voice rolled across the parade ground, "Ninth Regiment! Ninth Regiment, Fourth Platoon! Any men without guns, here on the double!"

At the mighty sound, people turned to watch a dozen of

11

our men running toward us. Pierce turned to Lieutenant Sheehan, "We're just recruits like I told Lieutenant Gere. We have never been sworn in, sir, but we'll fight hard if you have any more guns. We still need a couple of dozen."

"You'll get your guns. There's some in that magazine, still in boxes. They're calibre .59. Most of our muskets are .69. One shipment of munitions from Fort Snelling was of .69 calibre guns and .59 calibre balls. So you'll have plenty of ammunition. When you've transferred the shells for the fieldpieces, detail your riflemen to support Lieutenant Mc-Grew and his howitzer."

"Right, sir. But another thing. Sergeant Morgan, here, was with the artillery until he got shot up at Bull Run. Our men can handle a spare gun, if you'll put a sergeant in charge to make it regular. I've helped work a gun myself. I've heard that the Sioux are real scared of canister. We'll help anywhere we can to stop the devils."

"Jump to it then — and don't let the Indians get close to the guns. And I can depend on Sergeant Morgan to handle the artillery ammunition so we can get at it."

I was real pleased that he didn't hesitate to call me "Sergeant." Not having been mustered in had been a sore point with all of us. But he always treated us just like soldiers. As he hurried away, I saw that two of our boys were coming with the wagons. By now, the firing to the northeast was sharp and continuous. More Indians were forming at the lip of that big ravine, ready to charge in a body. It looked like they might reach the outer sheds. I fired all sixteen shots from my Henry .44 into the thickest mass and felt pleased that several Indians I had picked out dropped or spun around. But Frank's Sharps was booming at slightly longer intervals, and one of our boys kept saying, "You got the one in the headdress, Frank," or, "Good shot, Sergeant. The one in the white paint won't scalp any more settlers."

Then our wagons arrived and we climbed aboard for the run to the powder magazine. As we galloped away, I was watching a gray-bearded man they called "Sergeant Whipple" fire his howitzer. He wasn't in any uniform. I heard later that he'd fought in the Mexican War. They still called him "Sergeant." His shell went through the edge of the massed Indians and exploded out over the ravine. He must have cut the fuse for his next shot real short. That shell cut the tops of weeds on its way toward the Indians and exploded right at the lip of the ravine, where a new crowd of savages had gathered, ready to charge. A mass of bodies seemed to lift back into the ravine and out of sight. The closer fringe of Indians was being driven back by the musket fire of our Company B men.

Then we were beside the magazine, and Sergeant Bishop was posting his men to guard us against the Indians. He was a quiet sort, and his men obeyed his orders as though they liked him and had confidence in him, but they said he'd been a yelling, gun-swinging demon at Redwood Ferry when he had to break through a tangle of savages. Although his orders were quiet and firm now, his face was hard. He limped noticeably from the wound he'd received at the ferry two days before, but it was evident that he'd like another whack at the savages.

My men were laughing and joking as though handling powder and ball was a lark. They weren't even concerned about the crowd of Indians just beyond rifle shot to the west. I tried to sober them with, "Handle that powder real carefully, boys. And don't dent those balls when you set 'em down. Keep that canister separate." They worked more carefully, but fast.

Sergeant Pierce came out with an armful of muskets. In two minutes, six of our men had them loaded and primed. Corporal Hein came out with six more, and Pierce lined up his squad and marched them out from behind the magazine as Bishop's men fired a volley at a line of warriors racing across the prairie toward us. He'd waited until they were within musket range and stopped one rider. The others, more than a score, raced in on their quick little ponies. Frank's squad held their fire until they were less than a

13

hundred yards away, then ordered a volley. It stopped the charge like they'd hit a wall. Bishop's men got in another volley as they raced away. Several ponies were without riders. Before our men could reload, the Indians had picked up their dead and wounded and fled — but not all. I had time to aim carefully and squeeze off three more shots. I saw one Indian hit the ground and stay there. Even while he was calling the orders to reload muskets, Frank shot twice and brought down two riders wearing headdresses. It had been an expensive attack for the savages.

Frank waited until all of the men had reloaded their muskets, then he told Sergeant Bishop, "I think they won't try that again. I'd better trot over and support the Lieutenant with that howitzer. Looks like they're about ready to attack."

It took only another few minutes for the rest of us to empty the magazine. Going back to the bakery was a slower trip, for the ground was rough and I didn't want any cannonballs slamming onto bags of powder. Then we worked for nearly a half-hour stacking powder, canister, and balls ready for use. I was feeling better all the while, as our men proved they could work in spite of howling savages and screaming bullets. Not that any bullets had come very close while we were working at the magazine. Muskets fired from a running horse aren't apt to be very accurate — but they do go somewhere, and if you're killed by accident, you're still dead.

We tied the teams where we'd found them and I reported my squad to Lieutenant Sheehan. We found him with Sergeant Jones, who was rapidly working his six-pounder against the mass of savages breaking out of the ravine south of the officers' quarters. It was easy to see he knew his business. He was laying the gun himself, and the first shot I saw cut a wide swath in the massed Indians. Some of those knocked down stayed down. Others stopped to carry them back into the ravine. After two more rounds of canister, that charge broke up and the savages scampered back out of sight.

14

Sheehan issued muskets to several of my men, and detailed them to join the riflemen at the barricade who were keeping up a hot fire to protect Jones' men while they reloaded the six-pounder. Bullets from the ravine were nicking the stones of the commissary building and thudding into the barricades and frame buildings. A bullet splintered a post beside me, and I ducked as it stung my cheek.

Then there came a lull in the firing near us, and I could hear a new burst of fire to the north of the fort. Lieutenant Sheehan, beside me, had turned to watch it. "Some of the savages have gotten into that shed to the north where we kept our cows. Sergeant Pierce is doing a good job keeping them pinned there. God! If we can only keep those devils from getting up to our guns we'll have a chance." He said it like a prayer.

"Sergeant Bishop," he called. "Take eight men and these six with Sergeant Morgan and roll another six-pounder down beside Jones. He needs two guns firing alternately. Morgan has been in the artillery. You give him support while he works the gun," and he was off on another round of his defenses.

While I'd been busy, he'd put riflemen in all of the log buildings on the north and lined up our men behind the barricades near Whipple, who was defending the sheds to the northeast. Pierce's voice could be heard over the racket as his men reloaded by counting to support Lieutenant McGrew on the northwest corner. Somehow that bull voice gave me confidence that the fort's defenses to the north would be secure.

By the time I had a second six-pounder emplaced and firing, we'd been defending the fort for more than two hours. Only two or three men had been carried over to the commissary where the fort surgeon had set up his hospital. But more than a dozen men who were still fighting were wearing bloodied bandages on arms or heads. As my squad reloaded our six-pounder, I could study Jones' plan of defense. The Indians were massing for another attack but keeping under cover most of the time. As Jones' canister

15

went past them they would jump up and race toward us, then drop behind any cover or in a depression as he fired again. While he reloaded they would fire a ragged volley and come on.

Our Renville Rangers were firing from behind the barricade, but their muskets didn't seem to be any more effective than those of the Indians. Jones' men paid no attention to the bullets thudding into the nearby walls. My crew couldn't reload as smoothly as Jones' and I took longer to aim and fire. He slowed his firing to match mine. Presently he had time to wave encouragement. I was proud when he came over and noted that my men followed orders and paid almost no attention to the Indians' bullets. But on the other hand, I never saw *him* show the slightest fear.

Soon the wave of savages began to fall back with their dead and wounded. There had been little time for them to run forward as our canister was exploding among them at point-blank range. The next shells practically lifted them back into the protecting ravine.

But there was only a short respite from their attack. A fresh wave of yelling Indians raced toward us from all along the sides of the ravine. Lieutenant Gere's men ran over to stop a new angle of attack not in the line that our six-pounders could cover. There was a sharp engagement and for a few minutes his men were nearly overrun. Jones ran his six-pounder out into the open and blasted the Indians. He was in danger and I did my best to cover him. The hail of bullets became worse. Then his steady firing saved Gere's men, and Jones brought his gun behind the barricade.

In the next slight lull in the firing, a settler came over to us with a pail of water and a dipper. "My old shotgun ain't no use till they get closer," he said, "but I can carry water fer you fellers doin' the shootin'."

Others of the settlers came out with fresh baked bread and baskets of summer apples. Late in the afternoon a nice appearing woman they called Mrs. Sampson came out with soap and hot water and some bandages. Pain lined her face

16

and she hardly spoke as she bound up various wounds from splinters and spent bullets. We had been too busy and too scared of the Indians to worry about minor wounds. But she made us feel braver. Someone told me that she had saved her baby, but her husband and two of her children had been killed by Indians they knew, and had thought to be friendly. They had burned her home and she escaped in the night. Another brave woman, Mary Hayden, came out to help her. Tears had streaked their faces. Now, it seemed that they were past weeping. Their only thought was to help us fight off the savages.

The heat of the day passed and clouds piled high in the east. Finally, in the late dusk, there was no one for us to shoot at. The rattle of muskets died. For another hour we waited by our guns in alert apprehension. All the deeper shadows seemed to be peopled with savages. Occasionally a lone musket broke the new stillness. In the early dusk the crows had circled like dark clouds toward the woods to the south, then sped away, disturbed by the noise. Now they returned and were still cawing their way back to their rookery long after dark. Finally, a bugle blew the call that let me order my men to be "at ease."

Fort Ridgley, August 25, 1862[4]

Report of Lieut. T. J. Sheehan, Fifth Minn. Infantry: On Monday morning August 18th, at 10 o'clock, Mr. J. C. Dickenson reached Fort Ridgley from the Lower Sioux Agency, bringing the startling news that a wholesale murder of the whites was in progress at the last named place, this at first incredible rumor being a moment later confirmed by the arrival of other refugees bringing a wounded man. Captain Marsh at once resolved to go to the rescue. The long roll was sounded, the little garrison was promptly under arms, and hastily dispatching a mounted messenger (Corporal McLean) with orders to Lieutenant Sheehan to return immediately with his command

17

to Fort Ridgley, and directing teams with extra ammunition and empty wagons for carrying the men, to follow as soon as harnessed, Captain Marsh with Interpreter Quinn and 46 men marched for the agency, within thirty minutes of the first alarm, leaving at Fort Ridgley 29 men under command of Lieutenant Gere. Captain Marsh and Interpreter Quinn were mounted on mules. About three miles out the wagons overtook the command, and, placing the men in the wagons, Captain Marsh hastened toward the scene of the slaughter, meeting on his way scores of affrighted citizens fleeing toward the fort for protection. Only six miles from Fort Ridgley houses in flames, and mutilated but not yet cold corpses of men, women and children at the roadside, marked the limit thus far reached by the savages, and revealed the appalling character of the outbreak; but still in the hope that all this was the work of some desperate band of outlaws among the Sioux, and strangely confident that it was in his power to quell the disturbance, Captain Marsh, again forming his command on foot, hurried on.

At Fairbault's Hill, some three miles distant from the lower agency, the wagon road descended from the high prairie and crossing a small stream stretched across the wide bottom land of the Minnesota river, covered at this time with tall grass, to the ferry. Half way across this bottom, Captain Marsh halted his command for a moment's rest, and proceeded in single file, advancing in this order to the ferry-house, which stood on the north side of the road some two hundred yards east of the ferry landing. Here on the east bank of the river, on either side of the road, the heavy grass merged with the scattered thickets of hazel and willow, interspersed with open sand patches left by the river's overflow, one larger thicket extending southward along the river bank some two miles in varying width from twenty to two hundred feet. Across and close to the west bank were the high bluffs on which the lower agency was located, their steep face then covered by a thick growth of young trees and underbrush. Halting at the ferry-house shortly after noon, the boat was discovered to be on the east side in apparent readiness for the command to use for its crossing, though the dead body of the ferryman had been found in the road. Up to this time but few Indians had been seen, and these on the high prairie west of the river, south of the agency, on their horses. Now appeared some squaws and children on the west bluff of the river, and near the ferry was a single Indian who seemed marching as a sentinel. This was Chief White Dog, and Captain Marsh addressed him through his interpreter. White Dog said, "Come across; everything is right over here. We do not want to fight and there will be no trouble. Come over to the agency and we will hold a council." During this discussion two soldiers went to the river to obtain water for the men and discovered the heads of many Indians concealed behind logs in the brush on the opposite side. A drunken man at the ferry told the soldiers, "You are all gone up; the Indians are all around you; that hillside is covered with Indians." Captain Marsh then ordered the soldiers forward to the ferryboat. . . .

BATTLE OF FORT RIDGLEY, August 20-22, 1862

GENERAL: I have the honor to report that this post was assaulted by a large force of Sioux Indians on the 20th instant. The small remnant of Company B, Fifth Regiment Minnesota Volunteers, and the Renville Rangers, a company just organized for one of the regiments of this state, were the only troops I had under my command for its defense, and nobly did they do their duty. The engagement lasted until dusk, when the Indians, finding that they could not effect a lodgment, which was prevented in great measure by the superior fire of the artillery, under the immediate charge of Ordnance Sergt. J. Jones, U. S. Army, which compelled them to evacuate the ravines by which this post is surrounded, withdrew

19

their forces, and the gallant little garrison rested on their arms, ready for any attack.

During the night, several people, remnants of once thriving families, arrived at the post in a most miserable condition, some wounded — severely burned — having made their escape from their dwellings, which were fired by the Indians. The people in the immediate vicinity fled to the post for protection, and were organized and armed, as far as practicable, to aid in the defense.

On the 22nd they returned with a much larger force and attacked us on all sides, but the most determined was on the east and west corners of the fort, which are in the immediate vicinity of the ravines. The west corner was also covered by stables and log buildings, which afforded the Indians great protection, and in order to protect the garrison, I ordered them to be destroyed. Some were fired by the artillery, and the balance by the Renville Rangers, under the command of First Lieut. J. Gorman, to whom, and the men under his command, great credit is due for their gallant conduct. The balls fell thick all over and through the wooden building erected for officers' quarters. Still the men maintained their ground. The Indians prepared to storm, but the gallant conduct of the men at the guns paralyzed them, and compelled them to withdraw, after one of the most determined attacks ever made by Indians on a military post.

The men of Companies B and C, Fifth Regiment Minnesota Volunteers, aided by the citizens, did good execution, and deserve the highest praise for their heroic conduct.

I beg leave also to bring to your notice Dr. Muller, the acting assistant surgeon of this post, who, assisted by his excellent lady, attended the wounded promptly; and I am happy to say that, under his careful treatment, most all of them are prospering favorably. Mr. Wycoff and party, of the Indian department, with many other citizens, rendered efficient service.

Our small-arms ammunition nearly failing, on consultation with Ordnance Sergt. J. Jones, I ordered the

20

balls to be removed from some of the spherical-case shot, which with the balls fired by the Indians (many of them were collected and recast), was made into ammunition by a party of men and ladies, organized for the purpose, who worked day and night until a good supply was obtained.

The buildings composed of the garrison proper are still up, but they are much wrecked. All of the out-buildings, except the guard house and the magazines, are entirely destroyed. Most of the mules and oxen belonging to the quartermaster's department were taken by the Indians, and we are left with scanty supply of transportation.

I adopted every means possible in my power for the defense, by erecting barricades, covering the store-house with earth (to guard against fire arrows, several of which were thrown), determined to sacrifice all but the men's quarters and storehouse, which are stone buildings.

I also herewith inclose a list of the killed and wounded.

Very respectfully, your obedient servant,

TIMOTHY J. SHEEHAN,

First Lieutenant Company C, Fifth Regiment, Minn. Vols., Commanding Post.

Fifth Regiment: 1 killed, 9 enlisted men wounded; Renville Rangers: 2 killed, 4 men wounded.

(Recalled from Fort Ripley, Lieutenant Sheehan had ridden over 150 miles in 44 hours and commenced the battle of the 20th at Fort Ridgley without rest from that ride.)

Following Wednesday's Battle
We Dug In And Waited

Lieutenant Sheehan made another round of inspection of the outer buildings and barricades, and then detailed pickets to outlying points near the ravines. He stopped where I was cleaning my Henry rifle, and took the time to admire it by the light of a nearby cooking fire. "I've been watching you and your men, Sergeant. I'd like to attach 'em to my company. If Captain Pettit doesn't get the red tape straightened out, see me. How are you fixed for ammunition?"

"I've used up most of what I had, sir. It's too easy to keep firing faster that I can aim with a repeater."

"You weren't wasting many shots, Sergeant. And later on you were mighty fine support to Sergeant Jones with that fieldgun. You gave him a chance to work his gun slower and place his canister to better advantage. He had a hot barrel when you got there. I'll want to thank Sergeant

Pierce, too. He's a good man. His squad saved McGrew from hand-to-hand fighting twice that I saw. We'd have lost the fort if they'd gotten past him. I noticed something encouraging. Sergeant Pierce acted like he enjoyed the fight. I could hear him from all over the fort shouting encouragement to his men. And he handles that Sharps real well. He brought down a savage every time."

I was mighty proud of Company B. We'd had our first taste of fighting under fire and the boys had stood up well. But we had a tired, hungry squad of men that night. We didn't have to stand picket duty, but getting supper was a long chore. The shed we'd camped in the night before was a splintered sieve. Even our bedding was holed with shot and splinters stuck up like on a pincushion. Some of the blankets had been trampled in the hand-to-hand fighting when several of Pierce's men had fought off a bunch of savages. Whipple had acted promptly, putting a canister shell into the mass of Indians. Then our men had dashed back to the next shed and Whipple put a solid shell through the farther one. That had stopped the attack.

But now I was too bushed to eat. Frank Pierce took over all the work. He set a detail to getting supper, and another to gathering kindling for the fire. There was plenty of that. Then he was gone for a few minutes and came back with information about where we could find a tighter shelter for the night.

Some of Lieutenant Gere's men brought hard bread and beef and ate with us. Whipple's men counted off into two sections, half of them staying beside their gun while the others ate. He was called "Sergeant Whipple" because he'd held that rank in the Mexican War. To me, he seemed like an old man with lots of gray in his hair and beard — but he knew how to handle a howitzer and he fought as shrewdly as the best artilleryman.

Most of us expected the Indians to attack out of the darkness at any moment. It was their best chance to overpower us. Possibly they were more afraid of the dark than we

23

were. It was much later that I learned about their superstition about night fighting. The spirit of a Sioux killed at night can't see his way to the Happy Hunting Ground. I suppose that is as good an explanation as any. But we had a miserable night of it, staying awake and waiting for an attack.

I'd left my six-pounder under Sergeant Jones' care, at his express orders. He'd said there was no sense in all of us standing guard. So I told him, "I'll have my squad back early if we get any sleep — and on the double if there's an alarm."

"Better sleep inside if you can. It smells like rain."

Frank and I still had some wounded men to attend to. One of my men, Billie Hill, and one of Frank's platoon, Ward Davis, had bullet wounds. We helped them over to the stone commissary where the post surgeon had set up a hospital. He dressed their wounds, scolded them for not coming in at once, and cursed the savages who had attacked us. Ward had lost a lot of blood.

"We didn't have time to come over here, Doc. I'd rather lose a little blood than be dead. If those devils ever break inside the barricades we're done. Ow — wow!" and a yell he couldn't suppress brought sweat to his face as the surgeon probed for the bullet in his leg.

"You never acted scared," Frank told him and gripped his shoulders more tightly. Ward grinned and then fainted away. Frank let him lie back while the surgeon dug out the bullet and swabbed the wound. The wound was dressed when he came to.

Billie Hill had been watching the surgeon, and sweat beaded his lips. But his wound was only an open cut. The sting of the brandy that the doctor poured into it was the worst of his pain.

"I'll be all right tomorrow, Sergeant," he promised.

Frank patted his shoulder. "Come on back and I'll get you a cup of coffee and something to eat. Ward had better sleep here in the infirmary. You look like you need coffee too, Al."

"Fresh air will help," I told him, and we headed for the cooking fires. I breathed deep the fresh, cool, night air. Beside me, Frank drank the night air in sighing gulps as we tramped across the parade ground.

"That sawbones is a good man and we're lucky," he said. "Ward will have good care. Billie will be stiff for a few days but he can still fight if we need him. The other men who were wounded seem to be in good shape. Some of those settlers that the doc was treating had been burned almost past saving."

"He was helping them all he could."

"Yes, but I can't help but pity the Indians we shot today. They deserve all they got, but they haven't the least idea of keeping clean, and no medicine for treating wounds. After they get shot they just hide away until they get over it — or die."

But we had too much to do to worry about the habits of wounded Indians. We checked the sleeping quarters for our men, detailed men to look after the team of horses we'd brought, and then had time to eat. I sat leaning against the wall of the shed, listening. Several other men around me would suddenly hold themselves in that same motionless position of listening. A breaking stick or the crackle of the fire made all of us jump and turn. All but Frank. He was too busy. I suppose he'd been keeping an eye on his men all day. Now he had a word of praise for this one, for some special effort or skill, and he'd warn another man about taking better cover. He graphically illustrated how to lead a running Indian and how to aim quickly while using the barricade for cover and a rest for a musket.

"Make every shot count," he said. "As soon as you're on target, shoot, before the savage can get a shot at you. Between shots, just breathe deep and relax."

He noticed that I hadn't eaten. Presently he brought a plate of stew for each of us and sat beside me. He waved one plate under my nose and I suddenly realized how hungry I was.

25

"They're a fine bunch, Al," he said, and smiled until his fringe of dark whiskers lifted. His wide shoulders stretched the fabric of his old coat. Even when he sat with his stiff leg stuck out straight ahead his back was ramrod straight. Somewhere during the fight, he'd lost his slouch hat. Firelight glinted from the waves of his long hair. Like most of us in Company B, he'd left Freeborn in too big a hurry to get a haircut. Before we saw the next barber, we were shaggy as prairie ponies. More than half of us were growing beards.

I dozed and then awoke as a branch snapped in the dying fire. Some of the men were snoring quietly, or breathing evenly, but I had been too tired to more than doze. Even when I pulled a blanket over my shoulders, I had to raise up to pick out the splinters. About midnight it began to rain in torrents. That was one of the longest nights in my life.

This second shed was better cover than the first one, but it lacked much of being watertight. Fortunately, we were able to keep a fire going under the shelter of an old tarpaulin. Even that was a mixed blessing, although I enjoyed the heat. I was fearful that the light might attract the musket fire of the savages. Every few minutes someone would go out to the barricades and listen, and the rest of us who were awake would also hold our breaths and listen. About three o'clock some of the wakeful men volunteered to keep the fire going and stay on guard out beyond the firelight, so that the others could relax and sleep.

Toward morning I put on the big kettle in which we had cooked the wheat so the gruel would be hot for breakfast. That, with a cup of hot coffee, made us a meal that was filling, if not very tasty. Then as the cool breeze at daylight brought the fragrance of the meadow into our very cowshed, itself, I reported to Sergeant Jones with six of my men. He gave us explicit instructions about keeping the waterproof cover over the fieldpieces, and to be especially careful about the priming. His crew was already standing by a six-pounder pointing at the ravine. All of those not on watch went to work to build up the barricade. We didn't have to be urged. Death and torture had come too close to us on several occasions on Wednesday. We built a board fence between the officers' quarters and the stable, with holes to see through and logs to lie behind. Some of the settlers helped the infantrymen and the Renville Rangers to dig trenches and dirt banks for better protection where we had no material for barricades.

Billie Hill insisted that he could stand watch by a gun and I agreed to let him, but only after Doctor Muller, the post surgeon, had dressed his leg again. I looked in on Ward Davis. He was running a fever and hardly knew me. Several women were helping with the wounded. Most of the men with minor wounds were still out on the barricades watching. We were all busy. The drizzle was annoying only because it dampened our powder.

Cooking fires were going all morning for the settlers. The soldiers also seemed anxious to get food cooked and ready for another battle or a siege. With more than three hundred newcomers to the fort, food was getting scarce. Another beef was butchered out beyond the stable. Women were busy pounding up the new wheat to add as thickening to their stew. Most of the women worked even harder than the men. They seemed to feel that they had more to lose than merely being killed.

Lieutenant Sheehan appointed some of the settlers as a committee to get new families settled in the log barracks. There was astonishingly little trouble among them. Most of the harsh words I heard were to the children when they went on the rampage, yelling and whooping from one barracks to another. Half a hundred of them pretended to be Indians, banging with stickguns. The officers ordered them inside the barracks, but most of the older ones ran away instead, racing out toward the stables, through the officers' quarters, and even down into the big ravine. Somehow they thought the Indian raid was all over.

27

In the midst of the uproar, a picket out near the southwest edge of the prairie thought he saw Indians creeping up through the brush. He yelled "Indians!" and fired his musket. It was a false alarm — for which he was relieved of duty and reprimanded. I felt that he should have had a promotion. His alarm straightened out all the children. They fled back into the barracks and stayed there. Even though the men all raced to their posts at the barricades, we lost less time in the alarm than we'd lost chasing youngsters out of the way of the workers.

In the afternoon, the talk going around was mostly of wondering how the settlers could be escorted to Fort Snelling and across the Mississippi to safety. We had no idea how long the siege might last, or if it was over. The rider sent to Fort Snelling should have gotten back with a relief by Thursday. Lieutenant Sheehan had made the march from Fort Ripley in forty-four hours, farther and over much worse roads. It was our general opinion that the rider had been killed. The courier that had gone to St. Peter to overtake the Renville Rangers had brought them back within forty hours. (The Rangers had been organized by First Lieutenant J. Gorman from among the settlers up in the Yellow Medicine area, for service with a Minnesota regiment in the Tennessee campaign. They'd gotten as far as St. Peter when they were hurried back to protect their own people.)

No Indians were seen east of the Minnesota River on Thursday. However, some settlers who arrived about noon said there was a big camp west of the river, and that more Indians were riding in from the direction of New Ulm. Smoke had been seen in that direction. There were rumors that New Ulm had been burned by the savages.

Work went faster in the afternoon as the drizzle let up. There was good reason for our frenzy. Any relief would be too late if the Indians ever broke past the cannons worked by Lieutenant McGrew and Sergeants Jones and Whipple. We had no doubt about what would happen. None of the men would be left to tell about it. The Indians had been taking the women and older girls captive, the worst horror

28

they could imagine — if they lived to admit what happened.

The Rangers let the settlers help them deepen the trenches near the south line of buildings. Pierce's men found more logs for the barricades to the north and northeast. Wet earth was thrown on the roofs of the buildings. Some fire arrows had been put out with water on Wednesday. In the next attack we might not have time to fight fire. Toward evening, scouts coming in reported a far bigger gathering of warriors across the river. We could expect a much bigger attack — and soon.

But there was one order that pleased me greatly on Thursday. Lieutenant Sheehan put Sergeant Bishop in charge of the twelve-pounder and asked me to help serve it. Part of my squad under Corporal Cook continued to work the six-pounder for Sergeant Jones. One day of fighting had made them veterans.

Sheehan decided that the twelve-pounder should support all the other guns. We pulled it to the center of the parade ground and, under Jones' direction, practiced emplacing it to support him on the south, and then moving it to where it would support McGrew and Whipple to the northeast. We practiced emplacing it for an hour, swinging it from north to south, loading and aiming until the crew knew what to do. Sergeant Bishop marked out our lines of fire and warned Company C and the Rangers to keep out of our way.

Lieutenant Sheehan was a fine natural commander. He had been resolving hundreds of details, making decisions quickly and with intelligence. After practically no rest on Wednesday, following his long march, he had fought a great defense of the fort. Then he had kept the work moving on Thursday. He had encouraged both the soldiers and the settlers so that we worked with general good will. That was no little accomplishment. More settlers kept coming in all evening. Each one had his own tale of terror and his special need for help. To keep them calm and with a feeling of security, took the genius of a general and the humanity of a shepherd. Sheehan had both.

29

The settlers' committee found shelter for the newcomers. Doctor Muller tended their injuries. Some of them had been burned severely when the Indians set their cabins on fire — with them inside. With thoughtfulness, he put them in the care of the most capable settlers already camped at the fort.

Most of the settlers worked steadily to build barricades and help with the defense of the fort. They prepared food, fed the remaining horses, and milked the few cows.

Noting that we were getting low on ammunition, Sheehan put the older children to gathering up spent bullets along the stone walls and in the log walls. Each one was presented with an apple for his work. Some of the women were soon busy molding the shapeless slugs into balls for the .69 muskets, which was the size in short supply.

Pierce kept most of our men busy on the barricades to the northeast until dark. They had to tear down the sheds farthest from the fort in that direction. The splintered wood accumulated in the process kept the cooking fires going all day, boiling beef and potatoes and making wheat mush. We had very little of anything else. It was discovered in the afternoon that the two oxen still in the corral had been wounded in the fighting. Both were dressed out and we had a big meal of beef stew.

The determination with which everyone in the fort did their work spoke well for the courage of the settlers as well as the soldiers. Lieutenant Sheehan called together everyone who was not needed for picket or post duty, to tell us how proud of us he was. His speech went something like this:

"If we can keep those devils from getting inside the circle of cannons, we'll win out. You artillerymen did a great and brave job yesterday. Keep it up and there will be some promotions at Fort Ridgley. If we fail there'll be no one to tell of it — except the women and children those devils take captive.

"I expect every man to know what he is to do, and to do that job well. Settlers who just arrived tell us that there are hundreds of lodges of Indians near the Redwood Ferry. Our next fight will be hotter than the one yesterday.

"We will place another howitzer alongside Sergeant Whipple, to defend the north wall. Sergeant Bishop will hold his twelve-pounder in reserve on the parade grounds, to blast any Indians north or south. Keep out of his way. Keep all the children behind walls. If a cannon points your way, run like the devil was after you — or drop to the ground. We don't want any of us hurt. Eat hearty tonight. We may be too busy tomorrow. Be ready at the first sound of any attack. Thank you, and God help all of us to a better day. Dismiss!"

Even the women and children cheered when he finished — and were cheered by what he said.

Friday came on hot and muggy — like Minnesota gets in August after a rain. The morning passed too quickly for those of us working at raising the barricades. Every man found time to clean and grease his rifle or musket and check his ammunition. The grindstone near the blacksmith shop was singing all morning as men with swords sharpened them. It had been in use all day Thursday. Sergeant Pierce came over to where I was stacking solid balls, shells, and canister into the caissons. He gave me a bag full of cartridges for my .44 Henry.

"I found a man with a gun like yours, but the lock is smashed. A musket ball came that close to getting him."

"Thanks fella. How are you fixed for cartridges?"

"All of us who have Sharps still have plenty. We can't waste shots like you do."

"If I could hit 'em like you do there wouldn't be any savages left to shoot at," I said and he just grinned. Frank was one of the best shots on the firing line — or any line. He must have hit more than a score of savages during the battles at Fort Ridgley.

The worst alarm on Friday morning occurred when Lieutenant Gere discovered that we were almost out of water inside the fort. Sutler Ben Randall was supposed to keep a big water tank filled, but with over three hundred settlers using it, it was nearly gone. Lieutenant Sheehan detailed Company C to proceed to the spring in the south ravine, as a guard for the water wagon. A few minutes later two men came running back, calling for shovels and spades. The Indians had filled the spring with dirt and it was a big puddle of mud. It took an hour of digging by a squad of the settlers to clean it out. By noon the water tank was again filled with clean water. Luckily, no Indians appeared to disturb the workers while they were vulnerable.

But soon after the noon meal someone yelled "Indians!" The Sioux chief, Little Crow, with others that the settlers named Big Eagle, Traveling Hail, and Wabasha, three chiefs who had been supposedly friendly to the whites, appeared out on the prairie west of the fort. (These had all been farming on the reservation. Other settlers called out the names of the warlike chiefs, Shakopee and Red Middle Voice. Recognizing Indians they had befriended always drove the settlers into a storm of cursing.)

I ran over beside the twelve-pounder on the parade ground. Sergeant Bishop's men were on picket duty. He was urging Little Crow to come closer so they could talk. (It wouldn't have been a friendly chat. Bishop had been wounded in the ambush at Redwood Ferry.) Little Crow kept his pony well out of musket range. But he still demanded a parley.

At the first warning, Lieutenant Sheehan had called for the long roll to bring the men to assembly. As fast as platoons were accounted for, he sent the groups out to the barricades where they'd been on Wednesday. Sergeant Whipple ran his howitzer over to where it had a clear shot at Indians massed at the lip of the northeast ravine. Lieutenant McGrew placed his howitzer north of the long barracks where he could fire into the head of the gully. Single Indians came running in crazy zigzags clear up to the outermost buildings, as our pickets to the north fell back. A dozen Indians reached the protection of a shed and began to fire at Whipple from its shelter. The two howitzers spoke almost together. The shed lifted on its posts and fell in a tangle of poles, with the Indians underneath.

Then I heard Sergeant Jones' fieldpiece roar, and I knew that Company C and the Rangers were fighting off an attack from the nearest ravine to the southwest. Sergeant Bishop led his pickets back on the run to our western line of barracks and then came over to where I had loaded the twelve-pounder. "Can't we get into this, Sergeant?" I asked.

"Run it over behind Jones' six-pounder, boys," he said. A dozen shoulders shoved together and we had it rolling. The caisson came rattling behind us.

Jones' gun roared as we swung into place. "Fire while I load!" he yelled, and we did. As I expected, a score of savages jumped up from the shallow ditch ahead of Jones and began to shoot at the cloud of smoke still lifting from Jones' gun. I aimed at them and fired. Our men braced to hold the gun steady. Even I hadn't been prepared for the recoil of this bigger gun.

"That dropped a few of the devils," Bishop called out as I reloaded. Our smoke began to drift away. "They weren't expecting another shot so soon." His glee was short-lived.

"They're getting into the stable," Jones called to me. "Put a ball into it." I fired my load of canister at the mass of Indians and reloaded with ball, then aimed at the lower edge of the stable roof. Our guns roared together. The stable door blew inward, from his six-pound ball, and the roof lifted and caved in, from my heavier one.

I reloaded with canister cut to the shortest length of fuse, and it exploded just beyond the stable among the fleeing savages. "Do that again," Bishop said. "This fuse is longer. Try to catch that crowd by the ravine." Jones fired with our shot, and a giant broom swept the yelling devils into the ravine.

Now the stable was burning. There was a rattle of muskets and rifles, as a wave of Indians appeared farther along the ravine. Jones' six-pounder spoke. I saw the canister become a shower of black specks — the .69 calibre musket balls that had filled it. Then someone yelled, "Morgan, hold your fire."

33

I raised up from our frenzied round of "swab, reload, fire," and looked around. Sergeant Bishop had been pointing out what he wanted hit. I'd been working the gun.

Lieutenant Sheehan was slapping Bishop and me on the back. "Good shooting, men. We've pushed 'em out of sight for the moment. Your crew works like it had been trained for weeks. Swing your gun over to where you can support Whipple. He may need help. The savages are massing for a charge."

We wheeled the twelve-pounder over to the slight elevation by the bakery. Sergeant Pierce was vigorously directing the fire of his men on the east end of the northern defense. Between words of encouragement, he was squeezing off shots at the leaders. He saw us as his eyes swung over the defenses. One of his men came over to Sergeant Bishop. "There must be more'n a hundred up by the old magazine, just out of range of the howitzers," he said. "Sergeant Pierce thinks you might cut 'em up." His eyes were rimmed with red from the powder fumes, but his excited voice held no fear.

"We'll reach 'em," Bishop promised, and we were off on a run across the parade ground. We swung into line and fired one round of ball and one of shell canister with the fuse at extreme range. Both took effect as the Indians raced away to get out of range. Only a few stopped to pick up the dead and wounded.

In the meantime, Whipple and McGrew had chased most of the Indians attacking them back over the lip of the ravine. McGrew ran his howitzer out to the mouth of the ravine and fired canister down the length of the gully. His position was too unprotected to be held for long, so they raced back as Whipple fired twice at the savages coming out of the ravine. All that our crew could do for the next few minutes was to stand and watch. We had no clear shot at any Indians in range. Those out to the west were moving south in a body. McGrew was the first to interpret their action.

"They plan to join up with the Indians in the south

34

ravine, and they're out of range of our guns," he yelled, and ran over to ask Sergeant Jones what to do.

He was back at a faster run. "Help me with the twenty-four-pounder," he said, and our crew raced over to swing it around and load it. His first shell reached out to the running mass of mounted Indians and exploded among the leaders. The mass swirled as though it had been stirred with a giant stick. Ponies stampeded away, losing packs and people. As the remaining warriors hurried forward to join those to the south, we fired the big gun again. It roared like a clap of thunder. The two masses of savages had almost joined forces, and were racing toward us on a gallop when the second shell swirled them around like a great whirlwind. That deadly wind stopped all of them cold, and sent them scampering back to the nearest bank of the ravine.

Indians down in the head of the south ravine must have thought we'd forgotten them. Jones had not fired for several minutes. Now his fieldpiece spoke and a shell exploded on the near side of a group near the head of the ravine. Then he double-shotted his gun and the balls sped toward the edge of the ravine, kicked up a shower of gravel, and cut a visible swath through the mass of savages. That was the last attack of the day. Again we waited beside our guns until dark.

That evening our pickets counted seventeen bodies where the last two shots hit. It had been a costly attack for the Indians. For six hours they had made one massed attack after another. During the lulls in the roaring of the howitzers and the rattle of muskets, we could even hear a yelling chief, probably Little Crow, exhorting his warriors down in the ravine, urging them to destroy us so that all the land to the Mississippi would be theirs. What he planned would probably have come true if he could have destroyed Fort Ridgley. Then he could have swept over New Ulm, Mankato, and St. Peter — and all the settlements as far east as Fort Snelling.

We had no way of knowing when the next attack would come. The pickets tried not to get too near to the brushy ravines. They were clearly exposed out on the open prairie, while the Indians could hide in the brush. The Indians had first appeared out on the prairie, but we always discovered more of them in the ravines, where they may have been hiding and watching us for hours.

Lieutenant Gere had sent a courier to Fort Snelling after help on August 18th, right after that first ambush. We still had no way of knowing if the man had gotten through, or whether any troops there could be spared for us. Lieutenant Sheehan warned us to remain close to our posts. Since help had not arrived, we'd have to fight it out alone. And it would be a miracle if we could continue to fight off five or eight times our number of crafty savages. Again, we built our cooking fires inside the log buildings where the light would not expose us to the Indians. Now there were wounded to be taken to the bigger hospital set up by Doctor Muller and his brave wife.

This time we knew there'd have to be a burial detail. Two of the Renville Rangers and a rifleman from Company C had been killed defending Sergeant Jones' gun crew. How Jones' men got through without a scratch is hard to understand. The palisade we'd built in front of their log barricade had been shredded to slivers. Not a board at the height of a man was left unsplit.

I slept soundly that night — but not for long. I'd volunteered to relieve a sentry at midnight. We didn't need to man the fieldpieces. It would have been impossible to see in the darkness or to hit a target. Each man slept with his musket beside him. There were a few more guns for our men — left by the Indians who had died too close to us to be carried off by their brothers. When we buried them the next day, we saw where the Indians had been burying their dead. We counted over one hundred graves. No one dug down to see if there was more than one body in each grave.

Saturday was much like Thursday, except there was now a shortage of beef. We ate up all the beef that was left, and most of the potatoes. We were still tense with dread. Rumor said that more Sioux were coming in from the west. We didn't know if there'd be another meal, let alone a hot one. And we were short of ammunition. Lieutenant Sheehan had us point the twenty-four-pounder to the west in plain sight of the Indians. It might help to keep them at a distance, but we didn't intend to use it. It took too much precious powder. Sheehan put us to work throwing up more earthworks, and he posted many more pickets.

So far, our defense had been sufficient. But the fort was a shambles. Most of the buildings near the stable and south of it had been burned. Hardly a window remained in any building. The wooden buildings showed the chewing of bullets. We were short of shelter. The Fifth Regiment and Renville Rangers would have filled all the barracks. By now there were over four hundred settlers requiring shelter — and our men from Company B of the Ninth Regiment. A night and a day of heavy rain had soaked the whole area. The heavy twelve-pounder had churned much of the parade ground into a sticky morass.

It continued to rain part of every day or night. But that didn't stop the work. The next attack was too much in our minds. Barricades had to be built solidly between all the buildings left in the fort. Windows on the outer walls had to be boarded up. One of the favorite tricks of the Sioux in attacking a settler's cabin had been to creep up in the night and throw a lighted torch in through a window. By the light of the burning interior, they'd shoot the inmates. That could happen here in any of the barracks or cattle sheds used for shelter. All our effort was concentrated on holding out against any next attack. Each one had been harder to repel. The tension grew.

Rumor said that Little Crow was getting reinforcements from the western Sioux beyond the Missouri. Even the Winnebagoes, who were traditional enemies of the Sioux, had forgotten old hatreds and were joining forces against the whites.

All we knew for sure was that we had to keep the charging Indians outside the fort. One determined, successful

37

charge by them at any point, could reduce us to hand-to-hand fighting. In that we'd never stand a chance against odds of five to one. Only our artillery had kept them at bay. And only the steady and accurate rifle work of the infantry, rangers, and civilians had been able to keep the Indians from killing our artillerymen while they were reloading. It had been touch and go a dozen times in each battle. We dreaded the next one.

Lieutenant Sheehan had put every fieldpiece and howitzer into action. I heard him tell Lieutenant Gere of Company B, "Sergeant Bishop's crew was mostly new to the twelve-pounder, but they worked like veterans. Pick another crew and your best gunner to support McGrew with the spare howitzer. Bishop's crew will roll the twelve-pounder anywhere it's needed. Two guns firing alternately at each point will be more than twice as effective. In the next fight the devils may remember to charge in from all directions at once."

"How about more ammunition? We're still low on .69 calibre balls. Those Austrian muskets they sent us aren't worth a damn, but most of the ammunition left is that size.

"Melt down any spent balls in the logs. Draw more of the .69 calibre balls from the canister and replace them with the .59 we don't need. Fix bayonets on the Austrian muskets. If it comes to hand-to-hand fighting, the men working the guns may need bayonets and all the help from the settlers with shotguns that they can get."

Every night after Friday saw the fort in better condition to repel Indians. But each day showed a decrease in our food — and an increase in the number of settlers seeking safety in the fort. On Monday Lieutenant Sheehan assembled his men, "The couriers we sent to Fort Snelling may not have gotten through. I'd like two volunteers to leave at dusk, one to go overland and one down to Mankato and down the river." A dozen men stepped forward.

Sheehan picked two. And again we returned to frenzied work — and to wondering what would happen.

38

On Wednesday morning, a picket on the trail to the southeast called back to the next point that he could see a line of moving men. Five minutes later he was joined by the advance scouts and the outriders of the relief train. Presently, the main body of a regiment under Colonel Sibley came up with our pickets. Colonel Sibley had brought his forces to St. Peter and had spent several days in scouting and in gathering supplies. On Tuesday, one week after Lieutenant Gere's courier had reached Fort Snelling, Colonel Sibley made the decision to hurry to our aid as fast as riverboats to Mankato and marching overland could get them to Fort Ridgley.

Seeing those hundreds of men brought a mighty shout from hundreds of throats, and tears to not a few eyes.

Relief Finally Arrives

REPORT OF COLONEL H. H. SIBLEY, Fort
Ridgley, August 28, 1862:[5]

Repulsed in the attack made at New Ulm on the
19th, Little Crow . . . attempted the capture of Fort
Ridgley, and on Wednesday August 20th, knowing
the facility of approach afforded by the long ravine
to the east, also that the usual park of the artillery
was on the west line of the buildings, the main attacking party was moved down the river valley to the
mouth of the ravine, thence under its shelter to a
point opposite the fort, this movement being executed
under cover and entirely unobserved. To divert attention, Little Crow, himself, at about 1 o'clock P.M.,
made his appearance just out of range of the pickets,
on the west side of the fort, mounted on a pony, and
apparently inviting conference. Sergeant Bishop, at
the time sergeant of the guard, endeavored to induce
his nearer approach, but without success. At this

40

juncture the advance of the party approaching from the northeast was discovered by the pickets on that side and skirmishing commenced. Lieutenant Sheehan ordered the troops to form in line on the west side of the parade ground at the south end of the commissary building, facing east. By this time the Indians coming up the hill from the ravine had reached the level ground, and, driving in the pickets, poured a heavy volley through the openings at the northeast, gaining possession of some of the outbuildings at that quarter. Lieutenant Gere was ordered with a detachment of Company B directly to the point of attack, and moving at the double-quick, stationing Whipple with his howitzer in the opening between the bakery and the next building to the south; a detachment of Company C moved on the run around to the north end of the barracks to the row of log buildings, while McGrew wheeled his howitzer rapidly to the northwest corner of the fort and went into position on the west side of the most westerly buildings in the row. All these forces were at once engaged in a hard fight at close range.

The infantry, advantageously located around Whipple, kept up a hot fire, enabling him to work his gun to good advantage. . . . The men of Company C similarly covered McGrew's position and operations. McGrew first trained his gun to bear northeasterly, on the most northerly point at which the enemy appeared, and from which a heavy fire was coming; but his fuse had been cut for a quarter of a mile, and the first shell, though passing close to the grass, exploded over the ravine. Running his piece quickly behind the building, McGrew cut his next fuse to the shortest limit, reloaded, ran the howitzer out amidst a shower of bullets, and exploded his second shell in the very midst of this extremely troublesome party, wholly dislodging the savages from their position. The converging fire of these two howitzers, with their musketry supports, soon drove the Indians from the buildings they had reached and forced them back to the line of the ravine. The plan to capture the

41

fort in the first rush had been frustrated. Meanwhile, upon the attack to the east, the pickets in other directions had rallied on the fort, and Little Crow quickly closed in with the balance of his force on the west and south to divert the defense from his main attack. Ordnance Sergeant Jones, with his 6-pounder field piece, took position at the opening at the southwest angle of the square, supported by Lieut. Culver and Gorman, while the remaining men were posted in and around the various buildings and sheds in the most advantageous positions obtainable. Jones' position was particularly exposed by reason of the short ravine before described, up which the savages swarmed to easy musket range in large numbers, compelling him to deliver his fire under the most trying circumstances.

It soon became apparent that the Indians were in large numbers, with enough force to maintain a continuous siege, if so disposed, and that all the artillery ammunition was likely to be required, it was decided to remove at once into that stone building, from the magazine, the ammunition remaining there, consisting principally of the supply for the extra field pieces. The magazine stood in the open prairie to the northwest and distant some two hundred yards, the one quarter from which the Indians could not approach under cover. McGrew now took position so as to command any locality from which men detailed for this duty could be reached by the enemy, and the ammunition was all safely brought in. Little Crow's original intention and plan having met with such vigorous repulse on the northeast, the attacking force was distributed to all quarters, and the battle became general. For five hours an incessant fire was kept at the fort. The men in the garrison were directed to waste no ammunition and fired only when confident their shots would be effective, but found sufficient opportunity to maintain a steady return of the enemy's fire. The artillery did most efficient service in all directions throughout the engagement. At dark the firing ceased, but the men remained each where night found him, all in the momentary expectation of further attack by the wily foe. Little Crow had, however, withdrawn his forces to the lower agency. Rain commenced falling at midnight and continued throughout most of the following day. Thursday passed without engagement, and the day was improved by the construction of barricades, made of everything available, for the better protection of the gunners, especially at the southwest corner where Jones was in position. A 12-pounder field piece was manned and put in position in reserve on the parade ground under Sergeant Bishop of Company B; otherwise the officers, men and guns remained in the positions assigned in Wednesday's battle, and so continued generally during the remainder of the siege.

But Little Crow believing that Fort Ridgley once taken his path to the Mississippi would be comparatively clear, resolved to make one more desperate attempt at its capture, and on Friday, August 22d, his numbers having been largely augmented, a second and more furious attack was made. At about 1 o'clock P.M., dismounting and leaving their ponies a mile distant, with demoniac yells the savages surrounded the fort and at once commenced a furious musketry fire. The garrison returned the fire with equal vigor and with great effect on the yelling demons, who at first hoped by force of numbers to effect a quick entrance and had exposed themselves by a bold advance. This was soon checked, but from the cover of the slopes their fire was unceasing, while the very prairie seemed alive with those whose heads were clothed with turbans made of grass to conceal their movements. Little Crow's plan in this attack, in case the first dash from all sides proved unsuccessful, was to pour a heavy, continuous fire into the fort from every direction, exhausting the garrison as much as possible, and to carry the fort later by assault upon the southwest corner. To this end he collected the greater portion of his forces in that quarter, and, taking possession of the government stables and the sutler's store, the fire literally riddled the buildings at

43

that angle. It was found necessary to shell these buildings to dislodge the foe, resulting in their complete destruction by fire. Attempts were made to fire the fort by means of burning arrows, but the roofs being damp from recent rains all efforts to this end were futile. Still, in pursuance of the plan of battle, the hail of bullets, the whizzing of arrows, and the blood-curdling war-whoops were incessant. From the ravine to the northeast came an especially heavy attack, the object being to divert as far as possible the defense on this side, and here was some gallant and effective service again performed. Whipple from the northeast corner, protected in every discharge by the hot musketry fire of Gere's detachment and the men of Company C to the left, swept the very grass to its roots all along the crest of the slope, while McGrew, improving the opportunity, with most conspicuous bravery, ran his howitzer out from the northwest corner to the very edge of the ravine and delivered several enfilading volleys of canister down along the hillsides, practically sweeping the savages from their positions.

Now began the convergence to the southwest, the Indians passing from the opposite side in either direction. In moving around the northwest corner a wide detour was necessary to avoid McGrew's range, but the open prairie rendered the movement plainly apparent. Divining its object, McGrew hastily reported to Jones what was transpiring, and was authorized to bring out the 24-pounder, still in park, with which McGrew went into position on the west line of the fort and at the south end of the commissary building. Meanwhile the fire in front of Jones' gun had become so hot and accurate as to splinter almost every lineal foot of timber along the top of his barricades, but he still returned shells at the shortest possible range, himself and his gunners most gallantly exposing themselves in this service. During an interval in the fusillade Little Crow was heard urging, in the impassioned oratory of battle, the assault on the position. Jones double charged his pieces with canister and reserved his fire; meanwhile McGrew had fired one shot from the 24-pounder at the party passing around the northwest, and training his gun westerly, dropped his second shell at the point where this party had by this time joined the reserve of squaws, ponies and dogs west of the main body. A great stampede resulted; the gun was swung to the left, bringing its line of fire between the two bodies of Indians. Its ponderous reverberations echoed up the valley as though twenty guns had opened, while the frightful explosion of its shell struck terror to the savages and effectually prevented a consolidation of the forces. At this juncture Jones depressed his piece and fired close to the ground, killing and wounding 17 savages of the party who had nerved themselves for the final assault. Completely demoralized by this unexpected slaughter, firing suddenly ceased and the attacking party precipitately withdrew, their hasty retreat attended by bursting shells until they were beyond range of the guns. Thus after six hours of continuous blazing conflict, alternately lit up by the flames of burning buildings and darkened by swirling clouds of smoke, terminated the second and last attack.

During the engagement, many of the men becoming short of ammunition, spherical-case shot were opened in the barracks and women worked with busy hands, making cartridges, while men cut nail rods in short pieces to use as bullets, the dismal whistling of which strange missiles was as terrifying to the savages as were their fiendish yells to the garrison. Incredible as it may appear, during these engagements at Fort Ridgley the loss of the garrison was only 3 men killed and 13 wounded. Fighting on the defensive, and availing themselves of all the shelter afforded by the buildings and barricades, the infantry were admirably protected; while, as before noted, as each piece of artillery was fired the enemy were kept down by the hot musketry fire. The number of Indians engaged in the attack on the 20th is estimated at 500 to 600, and in the battle of the 22nd, 1,200 to 1,500. Their loss in two days could hardly have

45

been less than 100, judging from the number found buried afterward in the immediate vicinity of the fort. . . .

It was a battle on the part of the garrison *to prevent a charge* by the savages, which had it been made, could hardly have failed, as Little Crow seemed confident, to result in the destruction of the garrison and the consequent horrible massacre of its 300 refugees. It is but truth to add that no man in the garrison failed to do his duty, and that, worn by fatigue and suspense, and exhausted by loss of sleep, to the end every man was at his post bravely meeting whatever danger confronted him. The conspicuous gallantry of the artillerists was the theme of general praise, and the great value of their services was conceded by all, while the active and intelligent support that rendered their work possible is entitled to no less credit.

Post Surgeon Muller was active in attention to the wounded and ill, nobly seconded by his brave wife, who was, throughout the dark days, an angel of mercy and comfort to the sufferers, and who, with many of the ladies, admirably illustrated the quality of the most praiseworthy courage in the midst of surrounding danger. With the withdrawal of the Indians on the 22nd terminated the fighting at Fort Ridgley, the weary garrison could not be aware that such would be the case, nor for the moment relax its vigilance; hence the forces continued to occupy the positions to which they had by this time become accustomed. The construction of a line of earthworks on the south side of the fort was begun, the roof of the commissary building was covered with earth to prevent fire, and the barricades were strengthened as much as possible. Four more long days of suspense ensued, no word from friend or foe reaching the garrison until the morning of Wednesday, August 27th, just nine days after the first dispatch for help had been sent by courier, when Colonel Samuel McPhail, of the Minnesota mounted troops, and Wm. R. Marshall, at that time a special agent dispatched by

Governor Ramsey to hasten the relief of Fort Ridgley, rode into the fort with 175 volunteer citizen horsemen, having left St. Peter at 4 o'clock P.M. on the previous day, the advance of the expedition under General Sibley, whose infantry reached the fort on the 28th. Thus was ended the siege, and with it came . . . rest to the exhausted garrison.

General (Colonel) H. H. Sibley

To Governor Ramsey, St. Paul, Minnesota

The best part of Colonel Sibley's relief forces to us, was seeing Captain Pettit and Lieutenants Shaw and Hollister among the company. Shaw's men had gone to the relief of New Ulm on the same day we had come to Fort Ridgley. They had helped to drive off a big party of savages under Little Crow on the 19th, the day before he'd attacked Ridgley. Half of the lower town had been burnt down, but only a few people had been killed.

Also in the relief train were dozens of wagons loaded with grain that Lieutenant Shaw's men had been harvesting. All the grain available had been gathered in by Colonel Sibley, and that was one reason why it took him so long to come to our relief. (In the correspondence *to* H. H. Sibley they called him "Colonel." In his reports he signed himself "General." I expect he'd been promised the rank but it hadn't been confirmed.)

Captain Pettit had cleared away all the red tape. Ninth Regiment Minnesota Volunteers was a part of the Union Army. I was proud of the greeting Lieutenant Sheehan gave our Captain.

"In a way I'm sorry to see *you*, sir. I'd hoped I could attach Sergeants Pierce and Morgan and their men to my company. Their steady shooting and Morgan's work with the twelve-pounder held our lines a dozen times. There isn't a weak man in their outfits. Most of them fought like demons."

47

"And I'll be just as pleased to get them back."

"Find yourselves a camp where your company can be together. We'll talk later. Right now I have to write out a report for Colonel Sibley and get our new orders. I expect he'll want to move out against the savages right away."

Most of the afternoon was spent in setting up a camp for our Ninth Regiment over near the old magazine. And most of the evening was spent in swapping lies about how many Indians we'd killed. Shaw's men had had some hand-to-hand fighting in New Ulm. Two of Sergeant Tinney's men had been killed in a barn in the lower town. Their scalped and mutilated bodies had been found after the fight. A dozen of Sergeant Calvin's men had the biggest lies to tell. They'd fought in a burning house with five Indians and had killed all five, taking their guns and tomahawks.

George Peck was the only one of our men at Fort Ridgley to have taken the time to gather a souvenir. He'd been trapped in a shed out to the northeast of the fort when two Indians pushed in the door. In the moment of surprise he'd shot one. A lucky blast from Whipple's howitzer just then had driven off the other one. So George brought back a captured gun — rusty, worthless, but with a dried scalp nailed to it.

On Thursday night Colonel Sibley made us a short speech. I suppose it was mainly for the benefit of the settlers still there at the fort. He said, "We have enough men and artillery to completely wipe out Little Crow's band of savages, as soon as we can find them. We will make the frontier safe for all of you from now on. Our main forces will drive west with all speed to run down Little Crow. We will also send out smaller units of men and fieldpieces to establish a line of forts from New Ulm to the Canadian border. It will soon be safe for you to return to your homes and save your harvest. That is important. There is sure to be a shortage of grain and beef along our frontier. Make plans to go home as soon as possible.

"Otherwise, your only recourse will be to cross the Mississippi and stay with relatives and friends in Wisconsin or farther east. If there are questions, I will be glad to answer them. You can depend on us to do all in our power to help you."

It wasn't a great oration but it was well delivered, just as one would expect from the lawyer who had been the first governor of the state of Minnesota. The speech was also important to us in the Ninth Regiment. It outlined his plan for securing the frontier.

(During the early stages of Colonel Sibley's campaign[6] against Little Crow, Company B, Third Regiment, remained in garrison at Fort Ridgley. Lieutenant Sheehan left with Company C on September 18th, to join his command at Fort Ripley. Company B, Third Regiment, marched to Fort Snelling on November 9th, as part of the escort under Col. W. R. Marshall, accompanying the captured Indians enroute to the post. Uniting there with Company C, these two companies proceeded south and joined their regiment near Oxford, Miss.)

We Are Ordered To Forrest City

St. Paul, Minn., August 27, 1862[7]

Hon. E. M. STANTON:

The Indian war grows more extensive. The Sioux, numbering perhaps 2,000 warriors, are striking along a line of scattered frontier settlements of 200 miles, having already massacred several hundred whites, and the settlers of the whole border are in panic and flight, leaving their harvest to waste in the field, as I have myself seen even in neighborhoods where there is no danger. The Chippewas, a thousand warriors strong, are turbulent and threatening, and the Winnebagoes are suspected of hostile intent. The Governor is sending all available forces to the protection of the frontier, and organizing the militia, regular and irregular, to fight and restore confidence. As against the Sioux, it must be a war of extermination. The Governor needs six field-pieces complete, with horse equipments

50

and fixed ammunition; six 12-pounder mounted howitzers; arms, accoutrements and horse equipments for
1,200 cavalry; 5,000 or 6,000 guns, with 500,000 cartridges to suit; medical stores for three regiments and
blankets for 3,000 men. He earnestly asks that you
send these, or as much thereof as possible. I am
satisfied that I state facts correctly. Colonel Aldrich
is just in from the Sioux country, and confirms the
worst news.

JNO. NICOLAY

[John Nicolay was later the personal secretary of
President Lincoln.]

Two days later our Company B, Ninth Regiment, was
ordered to march north to Forrest City, to establish a post
for the defense of the settlers thereabouts. We arrived on
September 4th, only to find panic among the few settlers
still in the area. A skirmish with a small band of Sioux
at Stroud's mill, a few miles west of the settlement, had
resulted in the death of one white man and at least two
Indians. But the settlers felt that they had lost the fight.
All their cows and horses had been stolen by the Indians.
And three homes had been burned.

The Indians had been stealing horses in the area all
summer, but never more than one or two at a time. This
was the first attack on people, or any house burning.
These were Indians they had fed and befriended. The
settlers were thoroughly aroused. They came in a body to
see Captain Pettit, demanding the protection that Governor Ramsey had promised them. The leader of the
settlers, a bewhiskered German, Adolph Schlichstein, demanded the capture and punishment of all "renegade Indians" in the area. (At that time all Sioux were renegade.)

Two wagons had come to Forrest City with us to carry
food and supplies. Captain Pettit discussed the problem
with the citizens and then ordered Lieutenant Hollister
to take forty men and scout the area to the west of the
lake near our camp.

51

Lieutenant Shaw was to stay there on the east side of the lake and set up our camp and protect the wagons. Sergeants John Calvin and Del Tinney detailed the duties for the men remaining in camp. Sergeant Frank Pierce and I drew a blanket and forty rounds of ammunition for each man detailed for scouting, and two days rations. In less than an hour after arriving in Forrest City, we were marching out. The Indian War had come back to us in a hurry.

We were fully aware that this might be a long, hard hike. Without horses or scouts familiar with the local Indians, we had a slim chance of finding any Indians, let alone bringing back the stolen stock. But it would give us a good chance to learn something about the area to the west of Forrest City. We could expect forty or fifty miles of marching in the next two days. But I thought to myself, the men left behind to set up camp will be as tired as we are — knowing Captain Pettit like I do. They'll have little time to rest while building a fort.

The track we followed angled up toward a ridge. It had been pleasantly chilly on the march during the morning, but the afternoon had warmed up until it seemed more like July than September. We got to Stroud's mill about five o'clock and had the men fall out for rest and for filling canteens while Lieutenant Hollister and I went on up to the top of the ridge for a look-see. I'd been watching for pony tracks for the last mile. I had seen no fresh ones going west.

As our track curled over the top of the hill we saw what little the Indians had left of four farms. Three had been reduced to black and smoking sod walls and white ashes where the hay stacks had been. The fourth shack was still burning. A steady south wind was blowing black smoke away from us. The remains of a very dead cow was buzzing with flies. The Indians had not bothered to remove the skin after cutting out a haunch.

Then one of our scouts reported the tracks of a sizeable bunch of horses and cattle. He'd grown up on a farm, like most of Company B, and he claimed that the tracks were only a few hours old. Lieutenant Hollister sent a detail under Sergeant Pierce to find out where the tracks led. From the top of the hill, the tracks led off to the southwest as far as we could see. It was just possible that the Indians had camped for the night not too far away. Quite a few lakes dotted the wooded area to the west. Good grass was knee high in natural meadows.

Lieutenant Hollister looked at all the visible signs and added, "But you just look and come on back, Sergeant. Don't let them see you. And no fighting."

"Yessir."

The patrol had been gone only a minute before Lieutenant Hollister was leading the rest of us on a scout toward a little lake to the north. A man burst out of a thicket near it, yelling, "Thank God, thank God!" and waved his hat wildly. When he reached us he was too out of breath to talk.

"Where'd you come from?" Hollister wanted to know.

"I lived there," and he pointed to a burned out homestead. "Those devils killed my cow and shot Ben Sturmer. The rest of us holed up in a sod house to fight 'em off. We never had a chance. There were more than a dozen of the devils, all armed with rifles or muskets. When night came on, all my neighbors took Ben and the women and younguns and headed for Forrest City. I'd already turned the horses loose from the far end of our three pastures, into the timber, so I thought I could drive them toward town. The savages were busy cutting up my cow, but they saw me and I couldn't keep the horses running fast enough to get ahead of them.

"In the dark I slipped off my horse in the bottom of a thicket and hid out. They got our horses, all twenty-three of them, and seven cows. They was whooping and hollering most of the night. Probably found a jug of corn likker in one of the cabins. I was lucky. They didn't search my brush thicket. They seemed to be more interested in what they could steal."

"You'd better come back to Forrest City with us," Lieutenant Hollister told him. "I expect the Indians are long gone."

Just then we heard guns off to the southwest. Hollister said, "That's Pierce's rifle. He's in trouble. Come on!" and we lit out on the run.

We'd been stating out loud on all this trip that we needed horses. We really wanted them now. We must have run for more than a mile, hearing guns every little while. Four of my men were well ahead of me, struggling up a ridge on one side of a pretty little blue lake. We had little time to admire the scenery. The men ahead of me disappeared as they flopped down in thick grass. I slowed to a walk, and then on hands and knees, slipped up to where they were peering over the ridge. About a dozen Indians were racing their ponies in a wide circle around a clump of trees near the far end of the lake.

Then I heard Frank Pierce's rifle speak once more and an Indian's pony reared up and fell over. As the Indian hit the ground running, the rifle roared again and the Indian threw up his arms and pitched down on his face. Two muskets also blazed away from the thicket but they didn't seem to do any damage. I figured that the Indians were just out of musket range, but Frank could reach them. I hoped that their guns weren't any better than our muskets.

Now the Indians gathered in a bunch to wave their arms and scream. After some spear shaking they made a new circle in intervals that put them in position to rush the thicket from all sides. Someone beside me was whispering.

"I figure they'll dash in close from all sides this time, Sergeant." I turned and saw Hollister beside me. "Take your fastest runners and slip down this bit of a gully to that clump of sumac. When the circle of Indians gets near

54

enough, shoot as fast as you can. They'll likely be lying alongside their horses on your side, out of sight of Sergeant Pierce's men. I'll take the rest of our men and try to find the horses they stole. Since Pierce caught up with them they can't be far away. We need those horses. Maybe we can surprise the boys watching them. Keep these Indians busy for as long as possible. I don't want a big fight when we get to the horses."

Then he was gone. It didn't seem like more than a minute before we were crouched among the sumac waiting for the circle of attackers to get within range of our muskets. My .44 Henry would reach a little farther. I said, "Hold your fire until I tell you. Bill and Ed, you take the first one of those three. Tom and Perry, take the middle one. I'll try for the third. Load fast and hope for a second shot. Shoot high and lead 'em a little. Try not to hit any of the horses."

We all fired together. The middle Indian fell off his horse as though he was suddenly tired. I must have hit the third pony. He stumbled and came on. I fired again and his rider threw up his hands and rolled off his rump. The rest of the Indians turned away from us, then one of them rolled from his horse. The roar of Frank's gun came right after that. I expect he was picking off Indians again, just like he'd done at Fort Ridgley. Then we heard some shooting over in the direction Lieutenant Hollister had taken. That ended our battle.

All of the Indians still on horses raced over in that direction. My men ran for the clump of trees, calling to Frank and his men. I was pretty sure that Lieutenant Hollister would take care of his own skirmish long before we'd be able to get there. Frank looked mighty happy to see us, but he just said, "What took you so long? It's almost dark."

"Well, it was near sunset when we first heard any shooting. I supposed that you'd been busy shooting some ducks for supper. How'd you happen to tangle with the Indians?"

"They were watering a bunch of horses at the lake. We'd crept up close to see how many there were and a dog they had smelled us and started yapping. We tried to slip away but they had horses and soon overtook us. Peeks and Wilson were hit — bad — and we herded into this clump of trees to shoot it out. I got the varmint that shot Peeks. I'd like to get his rifle. It's a lot better than a trade gun. Help me here with Wilson."

He was trying to stanch a ragged wound in Dave Wilson's thigh. Then I saw that the blood on Frank's arm was his own.

"Here, Sergeant, let me see that arm." I ripped back his sleeve, then tore it off to make a compress on a three-inch gash near his shoulder. "Bill, you take Ed and Perry and go see if those Indians are dead. Bring in all their weapons. Frank's men can make litters for Wilson and Peeks."

All the while I was binding Frank's arm, he was holding a compress on Wilson's leg to stop the bleeding. He wavered once or twice as I dressed his wound, but he gritted his teeth and held that compress tight. By the time I'd patched up Wilson's leg the men had fixed up a stretcher out of poles and two coats to lay him on. All we could do for Peeks was to be sorry. He was dead. I saw that one of our men was getting sick, so I put his coat over his face to hide what was left of it.

Bill and the others came back to report four dead Indians and three dead horses. They brought in three trade muskets and a .55 calibre Spencer. Captain Pettit had been telling about the Spencers. Maybe I could get this one for him. I mentioned it to Sergeant Pierce.

"Seems like the Sharps is a better rifle than this Spencer, Frank, and you can't carry two — with one arm in a sling. I'll help you. It'd make a nice present for Captain Pettit."

"He can have it till we get out of the army. And thanks a lot, Al. If you boys hadn't gotten here when you did I'd never need any gun again. Those devils were just about to charge in from all directions. What else did you find, Bill?"

"Perry got himself a souvenir — some beaded leggings. I told him he'd better carry 'em on the end of a stick until he can scrub 'em with lye soap. They're lousy. We also got two feathered lances, and one Indian had this scalp on his belt," and he showed us a dried patch of skin as big as my hand, covered with long yellow hair. A dark scalp had been tied to one lance below the feathered tip. Probably it also had acquired lice. The Indians were seldom free of the parasites.

By now it was full dark, and both Frank and I were thinking about food. He was the first to speak. "Hollister must have had time to flush those Indians watching the horses, but I haven't heard any guns since you patched up Wilson. I expect that when the ones hunting for our scalps joined with the others, they stampeded the horses and got clean away on horseback."

"Probably you're right. Men on foot wouldn't have much chance," I said. "But the Lieutenant knows where we are. He'll be here soon, maybe. We may have to eat horsemeat steaks tonight. If we had a horse I'd chance sending a man back to report to Captain Pettit, unless Hollister gets back here pretty quick. If he comes, I'll let him make the report."

It was only a few minutes later that I heard a horse snort. I crept out into the lowest part of the gully. After a minute or so, I saw a horse's head against the skyline. I started to warn the others, then I saw the outline of a hat.

"Lieutenant, sir?" I called softly.

"That you, Sergeant Morgan?"

"Yessir. We're here in the clump of trees — all but Peeks, he's dead."

"Dead? My God, that's bad. Anyone else hurt?"

"Wilson has a bad gash in the thigh and Sergeant Pierce was shot in the arm. We dressed the wounds and fixed Wilson a stretcher between two logs. He won't be able to walk back to Forrest City. We'll have to carry him. Where are we to camp?"

"May as well stay here tonight, Sergeant. Those Indians are miles ahead of us by now. I don't think they'll be back. They must have taken nearly forty horses in that bunch. But when we first found the herd, we paired off and each pair tried to snag a horse. We got ten. Then coming back here, we saw a riderless pony, and one of the boys got close enough to throw a rope on him.

"Take a detail and bring in a ham off the youngest pony you shot. That'll make better eating after a hard fight than our iron rations. We've got a long patrol tomorrow before we can be sure there aren't any more Indians hanging around."

"I'll get us some meat, sir."

"Corporal Sterns, get a small fire going in the middle of the sandy area. Clear out the leaves and brush. We won't want any Indians to see the fire, especially with any of us in front of it for a silhouette. Cut firewood for morning. Send two men to the lake to fill all the canteens. After you've eaten I'll need two vounteers to ride back with a report to Captain Pettit. I'll write it out while you're eating."

"Here, sir," and several stepped forward. He chose two.

"Sergeant Pierce, you're in no condition to stand guard yourself, but detail eight of your men to stand guard by twos in two-hour watches. All you men off duty, sleep close to your guns, but don't anyone fire until you've identified your target. We're in Indian country, but there's no reason to go off half-cocked. The moon will rise in about three hours. We'll tie all our horses in here among the trees. They should be quiet in here. They've already had water and several hours of grazing. Now get busy. I'm getting hungry — for one."

Believe me, we all agreed. There was more than enough work to keep all of us busy, but we were still a little worried, for this was our first patrol. We were a silent

58

bunch in that clump of poplar and red oak. Some of the trees had been barked by bullets, and I caught the faint odor of red oak near the log where I sat eating my hunk of tenderloin. Red oak has an odor a little like watermelon — such as we'd feasted on, on the Sunday before we'd left Freeborn. In less than a month we'd been in two major battles. Now we might be close to a third. We had been shoved back into the war with a vengeance.

I moved over close to Frank. He was sitting with his back against a tree, supporting his wounded arm, in the sling, with his other hand, and looking white in the face in the dim firelight. My own old arm wound ached in sympathy, but there was nothing I could do about either one.

I'd known Frank for more than a year. We'd met in a first-aid station on that disastrous 21st of July, 1861, at Bull Run. He'd been shot in the knee. I'd almost lost an arm when a Johnnie Reb had jabbed me with a bayonet. We'd ridden in the same wagon back to a field hospital outside of Washington. The doctors wanted to amputate his leg but he wouldn't have it, even after the infection set in. I felt the same way about my arm. My wound began to heal and his got worse. He got so weak I even had to write letters home for him. Frank had been a big, husky man, all of six feet tall, and thick in the chest, until the fever took him down to skin and bones.

About the time he got better, I came down with typhoid and came close to the brink myself. They told me afterward that it was Frank's nursing that had pulled me through. We were mustered out of the army on the same day, to be sent home because we were still too weak to fight.

He'd urged me to go home with him to Freeborn, Minnesota, since I had no home of my own. I'd joined the Federal Army against the will of all my people. I still had too many Tennessee relatives and friends in Stonewall Jackson's brigade to let me feel right about shooting rebels. Captain Pettit was also from Tennessee, and I'd found

59

him to be a kindly and intelligent gentleman. More than sixty men had joined him in his first call for volunteers to fight with General Grant. Then he had been ordered to fight the Indians, and Frank and I hurried to join him. He was a patriot who preferred teaching to fighting but, as he said, this Indian uprising had to be put down. Frank and I had been given the task of drilling farm hands into obedient troops while we waited for definite orders and equipment.

Frank's family had made me feel right at home. I developed a great deal of respect for his brother, Hairston, (we called him "Hat"), who had served in a summer campaign against the Sioux in Nebraska in 1858. He'd warned us again and again about their treachery and had urged us to join an Iowa regiment headed for Illinois, if we were determined to enlist. But the reports about the Sioux uprising in Minnesota made up our minds. This fight was to protect our home folks. This was a call we couldn't ignore, even though I hated war with a passion.

Frank's sister, Susan, had been real sweet to me while I was at their place. Somehow I had hopes that we'd get together after the fighting was over. I hadn't cared much for Frank's wife, Caroline. "Carrie" was a constant nag. She was always screaming at him, and she had a hard tongue for all his friends. All she cared about was more dresses and fixing bows and doodads for Amelia and Alma, their girls about three and two years old. Frank was crazy about her so I kept my mouth shut. But I think he was glad to join the Ninth Regiment and get away from her for awhile. She was so selfish she spent more on frilly things for the little girls than Frank had been able to earn around Freeborn and then she harped on how poor they were.

Our seventeen dollars a month as sergeants looked pretty good to both of us, but Frank was foolish enough to promise to send his pay home to her. She didn't deserve it. She griped about the "danger of having another baby" and was so rabidly religious that she was always "improving" Frank and yapping about his stories, his friends, his love of hunting, and his admiration for Abraham Lincoln — whom she despised as uncouth and unreligious. Frank did not have a happy home.

While I lay there among our squads of troopers, that were friends as well, I wondered why other people couldn't get along together as smoothly as we did? We had shrugged off a lot of trials — rain, mud, and short rations — and our banter was still full of fun. And there in that bivouac in the woods, our sorrow for Peeks was sincere. They were the best friends I'd ever known. I needed every one of them and they needed me. Then I heard Frank get up and start on his rounds. Even though it wasn't his job, tonight, he had to make sure the guard had been changed and was alert.

Haze from off the lake was drifting through the tops of the trees and was made luminous by the slanting slivers of moonlight as the moon peeked over the hills to the east. I rolled over to a more restful position and the next thing I remembered was the faint light of morning.

Someone near me was letting his teeth chatter with the cold. I raised on an elbow and suggested that he'd better get up and build a fire. In a few more minutes five fires were glowing, and men were huddled near them, still wrapped in their blankets. Now that it was time to get up I dropped off to sleep. A horse snorted as Lieutenant Hollister, both hands cupped around a steaming cup of coffee, came past the area where they'd been tied. He looked tired, as though he'd slept little.

"Eat your breakfast, men. Refill your canteens and be ready to march in one hour," he said. "Morgan, detail six men for scout duty. Two ahead and two on each side. They'll ride the horses we recovered from the Indians. That will leave two for Pierce and Wilson. They've lost enough blood to make riding a necessity. And I noticed that Pierce has been up in the night, several times, checking the guard. That's more than you were ordered to do, Sergeant. I appreciate it."

61

"I couldn't sleep, sir, but I feel all right."

"How about you, Wilson?"

"I'll be glad to get a ride, sir. My leg burns and it's stiff, but I can sit a horse."

"I'd send you back to camp if I could spare the guard. We'll follow the trail of the Indians to see where they're heading. Then we'll swing north and see if we cut the trail of any others. Your scouts in front and on the left will have the most riding to do. Keep in sight of us as much as you can. Report back to me if you see any Indian sign — or any settlers still out here."

The scouting tour was a monotony of mosquitoes and scenery. It was pretty country. Some lake was always in the picture. In the afternoon we crossed the Crow River and followed the ridges north of it back to Forrest City. There'd been no sign of Indians after we left their trail that morning. It had kept straight on. From the top of a hill we had seen it more than a mile to the southwest. Then we'd swung north, passing several sod and stone settler's cabins. All were deserted. All had been broken into and looted. Only one had been burned. The only white man we saw on the whole patrol was the one near Stroud's mill, and he had scurried away at the first sound of firing.

We marched into camp in Forrest City just as the other men were eating supper. They didn't even wait to finish eating before they were demanding to know all about our patrol.

"Captain Pettit told us you had a battle and Peeks was killed and Wilson and Sergeant Pierce shot."

"That's right. There was a dog with the Indians. They smelled our scouts, and the Indians caught us before we could run to cover. We ought to get ponies for scouting."

"It was lucky that any of you got away. How many were there?"

"About a dozen. We shot four. And got back some horses."

"Do you think they'll be back?"

"Probably. If they think there's anything else to steal. We only saw one settler. I expect he came back here."

"That must have been old Tom Schuler. He got in last night and said you were in a big battle with more than fifty Indians that had chased him before and stole his horses. He wanted Captain Pettit to go out in force and bring 'em back."

"Fat chance catching Indians with foot soldiers!"

"Well, we shook 'em up a little and followed their tracks for a few miles. They're out of the county by now. But that was just a skirmish. Sergeant Pierce's Sharps was more than a match for 'em. *Those* Indians will be more careful next time."

By then, Perry was showing the beaded leggings, and Pierce was cautioning him again to scrub them with lye soap to kill the nits and lice. (He did, but not soon enough. He found lice in his shirt and then *we* scrubbed *him* with lye soap and dunked him in the far end of the lake.) Bill displayed his captured spears and the scalps. That sobered the bunch of them.

Frank Pierce gave a stern look around and said, "When old Tom Schuler told you we were being murdered why didn't you come to help us? Fine bunch of cowards you are!"

"We got ready to march immediately — within a couple of hours. Then the Lieutenant's message came saying you were all right except for Peeks and were going to continue the patrol. We were afraid we'd miss you. If you came back to Forrest City and didn't find us you'd have probably gotten scared and gone home."

"Aw, you didn't even care. We had to run all the Indians out of the country by ourselves. Schuler never saw all of 'em; there must have been a hundred — maybe five hundred," and Perry did his best to keep his face straight and look stern and brave like the conquering hero.

But in spite of the banter, most of us knew that fighting Indians was going to be a long hard campaign — on foot.

63

Captain Pettit had actually kept all the men in readiness to come to our relief if we'd met a larger party of the renegades than we could handle. He'd also used the danger as an excuse for setting up log barricades to make the post secure against a possible Indian attack. They'd worked all day cutting trees for enough logs to surround the wagons and our supplies. As I'd expected, Lieutenant Shaw's men were as tired as we were, even after two long days of marching.

In the next few weeks I worked harder than I'd ever worked in my life. We built a barracks and stable of heavy logs to house our supplies until we could build a warehouse. Captain Pettit slept in a tent just as we did. The barracks was his office and was used as a cook house. His tent stood at the head of our double line of army tents, eight on a side, eight men in most tents. We four sergeants had a tent to ourselves.

The next log building was a kitchen and bakery. By the time snow stayed on the ground, we were able to move all our equipment into the barracks, but we still slept outside. By then we'd put up a sizeable post, both for defense and as a warning to any Indians who might still be roaming within twenty miles of us. Rumor had it that we'd soon build a new post at Sauk Centre and possibly one in between.

One wagon train had passed through Forrest City in September from Fort Snelling on the way to Alexandria and Fort Abercrombie on the Red River of the North. The drivers and guard stayed overnight at our post, and we kept them talking most of the time they were there. They had a recent newspaper that we took turns reading out loud to the others. It was all about our Union victory at Malvern Hill and our defeats ever since. We had a new commanding general in St. Paul. Major General John Pope had reported a victory at the Second Battle of Bull Run — only to find General Robert E. Lee flanking his left. Pope was forced to retreat to Washington and was sent west to lick his wounds. McClellan was out of favor

64

with the War Department, but President Lincoln was giving him a chance to show what he could do. If he could fight like he could organize an army and get supplies, the rebels would soon be licked. At least the paper made it sound hopeful.

Our worst problems at Forrest City were with the settlers. At least once a week a delegation would come over and demand that we go out and recover stray horses and cattle that they were too scared to go after. We got most of them back. Also, we saw a few Indians who promptly skedaddled to the west. Our presence in Forrest City was all that kept a few settlers still there — that and their lack of transportation to Wisconsin.

The Shooting Match

Forrest City[8]

Dear Sister: The Indians made the attack some time before daylight, yelling and hooting as they came. The Indians burned four houses and took 50 or 60 horses and such other things as they liked. Two men were wounded. There are a number of houses burned around here and some good ones. The inhabitants have all left their farms. Some have gone to the large towns on the river and some have concentrated in the small towns all very much disheartened . . . The boys enjoy themselves well. Edward Patterson, Allen Morgan and I tent together. It takes sixteen tents to hold us all and they are arranged in two rows with the Captain's tent at the head in the center. . . . I also saw Tellif Myrick of the 3rd Regiment and Henry and William Velie. They are all well.

Yours forever,
Frank B. Pierce

Then about the end of November, several platoons of the Third Regiment Minnesota Volunteers stopped over at Forrest City on the way back to Fort Snelling. I'd known that a Freeborn boy, Tellif Myrick, had joined the Third and sure enough Frank and I found him and had time for a talk.

"Fort Abercrombie must be clear out in the Indian country, Tellif. Weren't you scared of the Sioux? I heard that there were thousands of warriors up on the Yellow Medicine."

"The Sioux are raiding farther south. That is Winnebago country. And we saw a few Chippewas. Looks like you've been working like mad around here. What's the long building?"

"That's the warehouse. We're a stopping point for wagon trains going to Alexandria and on west to your post. Our only 'fort' if we're attacked is the log barracks, but with the log corral and the stable we have three sides of a square protected. The lake on the west is open. Anyone coming around it has to cross the meadows. We'd likely see 'em."

"Looks like you've cut all the trees within musket shot, and cut the stumps too low to give cover. What did you leave the three big oaks by the barracks for?"

"Shade, mostly. We use 'em for a lookout sometimes."

"And does the Captain let you swim in the lake?"

"Sure. We sank a well that pumps water inside the barracks. But the only ones still crazy enough to go swimming are Al, here, and Sergeant Del Tinney. They have a bet on about who can keep it up the longest."

"Del always was a warm-blooded cuss. Swims like a seal."

"So is Al. How did you like Fort Abercrombie?"

"I was glad to leave," and Tellif grinned. I thought I could stand cold as well as most, but it's always blowing — mostly from the north. I was on the wood detail. We cut logs for another barracks and a warehouse same as you have. Our square is covered with almost as much bark and chippings as yours. Before we got up there, they'd built a stables for the officers' horses. I wish we had some."

"Our officers bought their own. That's why we cut wild hay," and I pointed to the big stack by the corral. "Frank wrote home about a fine pony he'd bought from his brother, but they won't let us enlisted men have personal horses. We can only have the equipment issued to us. An officer can buy his own uniform, sword, and side arms and his own horse. We sure need horses."

"We heard you'd had a couple of bad raids at Abercrombie. A Captain Van der Horck came through, soon after we got up here. He had his arm in a sling. Said he'd been shot in the battle of September 3rd. He said the Indians had all but captured the fort on that raid."

"That was before I got there. Our Captain Burger took over from Van der Horck about the middle of September. He was sick in bed with a wound in his arm. The post surgeon said his wound was infected and wanted to amputate but Van der Horck called him a bloody sawbones. They had a row about it.

"Van der Horck got mad and put his men to digging trenches again in two hour watches digging and two on guard duty. They had almost no chance to sleep. That's how he got shot in the first place. He tried to run the fort like a Prussian officer. When things didn't please him he'd load on the work.

"The Indians had run off about two hundred head of cattle and most of their horses and mules on August 30th. He put the men to digging trenches and building revetments on the open sides of the fort. He and a staff officer would sneak around the post trying to catch the pickets asleep. A sentry thought he saw Indians slipping in by the corral and called a warning. Van der Horck tried to drop down out of sight. The sentry fired.

"He tried to have the sentry courtmartialed and shot for assaulting an officer, but all the other officers and men were sticking up for the sentry. The final report was that the sentry had 'fired in the line of duty.' It was a good thing he shot Van der Horck. The Indians were closing in for a raid, but the other pickets were alerted and held 'em off until the fort was aroused and could fight 'em off.

"Anyway, the sentry was the pet of the Fifth Regiment when we got up there. That could have been a massacre."

"But didn't the sentry recognize Van der Horck?"

"I have a hunch he knew who it was. Maybe he just wanted to make him quit sneaking around in the early morning. And with the Indians raiding, he may have been a little quick at shooting. The staff officer admitted that Van der Horck hadn't answered the sentry's challenge. The Captain claimed that he hadn't had time. When we got up there the men were hoping Van der Horck would start prowling around the post again. They claimed they'd hit more than his arm next time."

"Jerusha, he must have been a bugger!"

"Like I said, they were glad to see us when we got there. We had three howitzers with us. Lieutenant (Robert J.) McHenry was in charge of the artillery. He made some changes in the placements old Van der Horck had dug, and the old Dutchman chewed him out for that. So our Captain Burger suggested that Van der Horck ought to go to Fort Snelling and get his arm looked after. We haven't heard any more about it."

"He didn't look happy when he came through here."

"He always looked angry about something. I think Captain Burger sent dispatches to Colonel Sibley at Fort Snelling about the whole matter. Anyway, they dropped it."

"Have there been any more raids on the fort?"

"Only a few skirmishes. After they got most of the cattle and horses back, the Indians tried to raid the detail set to guard them while they grazed. Last week the pickets traded a few shots with two small bands of renegade Winnebagoes.

"They are blood enemies of the Sioux that were raiding around there around the end of August. The Sioux were all called back to help Chief Little Crow fight the settlements to the south. We've seen a few Chippewas around Fort Abercrombie, so I don't think the Yanktonais and Santees from Dakota Territory are still about. The Chippewas made a raid at Georgetown. That's down the Red River of the North about fifty miles, at the Agency. There's a warehouse there for annuity goods, but the people killed there were at a hotel."

"Wow! I'd hate to be stuck up there, clear off the map. What is there besides renegade Indians?"

"Trappers. A lot of the supplies for the Hudson Bay posts go down the Red River of the North to Winnepeg, and then on to other Canadian trading posts. When the river froze, almost all travel stopped. They didn't need us any more. But Fort Abercrombie is an important post, especially in summer."

"Where is your company going, now?"

"Down to Fort Snelling to join our regiment. The Third has orders to go down and settle the fighting near Nashville. General Grant has a bear by the tail and can't let go."

Frank's eyes lit up at the talk of a fight. "We don't get any news till it's a month old. But I heard he's tearing into the rebels. Even when he's half-licked he comes back harder and stronger. Give the rebs a shot for me.

"But we may have some hard fighting up here, when warm weather comes. Have you heard anything about a campaign to the west, to punish the Sioux for the massacres?"

"Not up there in the backwoods. Who's going to guard the Minnesota frontier?"

"Rumor says that Colonel Sibley has gathered in most of the repentant Indians and saved the white captives. Now he's going to chase the Sissipapas and Brules back across the Missouri River, so there won't be any renegades left here."

"There's a lot of bad Winnebagoes and Chippewas. We were getting rumbles about the tribes north of the Mississippi. They're making big talk on the reservations north of Fort Ripley. The young bucks are breaking out in bands

70

too big to be merely hunting and trapping. If they should happen to have a hungry winter, they'll make plenty trouble in the spring after the grass is tall enough to fat up their ponies."

"And what have you been doing besides building up a post?"

"We went as guard to a train of forty wagons a few weeks ago," I told him. "Lieutenant Hollister took twenty-five men and we went on through Sauk Centre to Alexandria. We saw a few Indians. They turned out to be a family of Winnebagoes on the way home from harvesting wild rice. We gave them enough meat for a big meal, and they were peaceable enough.

"But we watched our blankets and guns. The settlers' big complaint has been that the Indians would beg a meal, eat it, and then attack. Settlers at Fort Ridgley pointed out Indians in the attacking party that they had fed and befriended only a few days earlier. Indians are friendly only when they are hungry."

"It's been the same up on the Red River. They stole most often from people they knew."

We enjoyed that talk with Tellif. But it was all too short. We had to get busy with camp duties. I was in charge of the guard that night. Frank drew rations for both platoons. Someone at the commissary remarked that Frank had a fine rifle and was a crack shot with it. The men from the Third claimed that no one could outshoot their Sergeant Ryan. In a little while the boasting got to be noisy. Lieutenant Hollister went over to quiet things down.

"Don't argue, men. Come daylight we'll set up some targets and soon know who can shoot. We've got a dozen men here in Company B of the Ninth who will be hard to beat."

Then someone in the Third told us to put up some money where our mouths were and we had to cover their bets. Fortunately we'd been visited by the paymaster the week before. The officers set up some rules and, at the in-

71

sistence of the visitors, a rally of quick firing was included, with offhand and armrest shooting. I went over to chat with Tellif with the idea of finding out what kind of rifle Sergeant Ryan used. He had two rifles, a Sharps .45 for accuracy and a .44 Henry like mine for quick firing. I hurried back to Frank.

"You'd better borrow my rifle for the quick firing, Frank."

"I've never used it but once. I prefer accuracy."

"I know. But you're pretty good at offhand shooting. Let's go try a few shots with my Henry. It's almost dark, but you can get an idea where and how it shoots."

We went down to the shore of the lake, where there were a few men still shooting at corked bottles and pieces of wood out a few rods. Frank threw a sizable chip of bark way out into the water and began to fire my gun as fast as he could work the lever. Every shot made the chip dance. I'd have been burning with envy if I hadn't admired him so much. It was better than I could do, and I was used to my gun. I had him reload the magazine and he began shooting as fast as before, but at the tiny bits to right and left. A group that was watching gasped as the last of ten shots turned the last piece to dust.

"No wonder the Ninth put up their money so fast."

"Yeah, that's good shooting. He aims quick but he's slow on reloading. Sergeant Ryan is a lot faster."

I didn't say anything. Frank and I walked back to our tent. "That'll give 'em something to think over," I gloated. "Maybe they'll hedge their bets a little."

But nothing seemed to dampen their assurance. Some of them even offered odds on Sergeant Ryan. The bragging about the crack shots in the two regiments kept the camp-fires burning far into the night. I made the rounds of my sentries and warned them to look out for any visitors who might take to wandering around camp in the dark. "Don't shoot any strangers without a second challenge. Save them for Fort Snelling."

72

"We'll be careful, Sergeant," one picket told me. "They have some money we want. I can't collect off a dead soldier."

The next day, Sunday, was clear and cold enough to crisp the grass and stiffen the ground and the trodden snow. It might be a little slushy later. Most of the morning was spent in a dozen shooting matches by individuals and teams. Scoring took the most time. We were lucky to break even in the team shooting. Frank had trained several of his squad to be good shots, but the Third Regiment had enlisted some trappers who were experts with the new rifles.

Sergeant Ryan was no match for Frank at either offhand or armrest shooting. Two of the trappers outshone any on our team. The scoring was still even when, in the final contest, Sergeant Ryan set up two rusty tin plates at sixty yards and declared he could put ten shots in his plate ahead of Frank.

I'd never seen anyone shoot a Henry so fast. In sixteen shots he put nine in his plate. His friends were commenting that he must be nervous, or he'd have done better. Frank was firing slower and steadier. I counted three in, then a miss, four more in the plate, a miss, and again four near the center. Ryan had thrown a shell into the chamber of his Henry and fired again with Frank's thirteenth bullet. A judge ran back with the plates. Few of us had ever seen such shooting.

"Eleven shots in the plate out of thirteen," Ryan murmured. "And well grouped. I was beat even before you fired your last shot. Man! I'd like to hunt Indians with you."

He took losing the match with better grace than some of the others took losing their money. There might have been more than sharp remarks, but just then the mess call rang out and we all trooped off to the special Sunday dinner the cooks from the several platoons had prepared. There the talk drifted to the fighting that our company had done at New Ulm and Fort Ridgley, and what the Third had done at Fort Abercrombie. They also had a lot to say about what they'd do at Vicksburg — if they got there. (Some of their

73

bragging came true. The Third Regiment Minnesota Volunteers made a great name for themselves there — along with the Fifth and Seventh.)

REPORT OF CAPTAIN EMIL BURGER, Fort Abercrombie,[9] Company D (Third Regiment Minnesota Volunteers) Capt. John Van der Horck was mustered into service March 15, 1862, and was ordered the same day to proceed to Fort Abercrombie, D. T. to relieve the troops stationed there. The company arrived on the 29th of March and Captain Van der Horck took command. . . . Upon the arrival of the treaty commision at St. Cloud the report of the Indian outbreak reached them. . . . A courier was immediately dispatched to Mr. Thompson, who was in charge of the treaty train . . . and to Lieutenant Cariveau to return with his command to the fort. . . . As soon as news of the outbreak reached the fort the garrison began to construct earthwork, fortifications of hewed logs, etc. When the detachment from Georgetown arrived, ten men under Lieutenant John Groetch were detailed to reconnoiter as far as Breckenridge (a distance of fifteen miles) . . . inmates of the hotel, three men, a woman and a child, had been murdered and terribly mutilated. . . . About the 29th of August a good protection had been provided, and in the bastion of the work on the southwest corner of the garrison there was placed a 12-pound howitzer. . . . Another howitzer was placed in a log house to protect the north and east sides of the garrison, and also as a defense against an attack from Slab Town, the old site of Fort Abercrombie. A third howitzer was placed near the men's quarters. These three pieces were manned by experienced men of Company D, who had been in the artillery service in Germany. About 2 P.M., August 30th, a party of Indians appeared within a mile of the fort, near the Wild Rice river, and drove off a herd of stock grazing in the vicinity. . . . The following morning a detachment was sent out to recover the stock, if possible, and returned in the

74

evening with about forty head. The Indians made no demonstrations for several days, except to watch our movements from the thick underbrush across the river. The work of the fortifications was continued. The men were much exhausted, half of them being on guard during the day while the other half worked on the breastworks. During the nights the whole command was on guard, half being on post at a time, the relief occurring every two hours. It was feared that the men thus tired out would relax in their vigilance, and to guard against this, the officer of the day made the rounds at night every two hours and the commanding officer visited the guard and post every night, usually before daybreak. On the 3rd of September, Captain Van der Horck and the orderly sergeant inspected the outside picket line, between 4 and 5 o'clock, as usual; on reaching the last post of the line, the guard, mistaking the party for Indians, fired. The shot wounded the captain in the right arm. The guard in explanation, claimed that he had seen Indians crawling near the line during the night. At daybreak, an hour later, while Dr. Brown was dressing Captain Van der Horck's wound, the Indians attacked the post from the south side in large force. First Lieutenant Cariveau being sick, Lieutenant Groetch was ordered to take command of the post. The fight lasted from 5 to 11 A.M., when the Indians were repulsed and retired to their camp south of the fort. It was estimated that over 400 warriors participated in the attack. Many of the Indians were killed and wounded, the loss of the garrison being but two, Corp. Nicolas Hettinger wounded in the right shoulder and Private Edwin D. Steele in the abdomen, of which he died September 7th. After the fight was over and the Indians had retreated, it was ascertained that there had been but 350 rounds of musket ammunition left in the garrison. The arms in the hands of the men were the Harper's Ferry muskets, caliber 69, and on leaving Fort Snelling the command was furnished with only 2000 rounds of ammunition, the company commander being told that there were 40,000 cartridges at Fort Abercrombie. On examination, however, it was found that these cartridges were 58-caliber. This discovery was made in April, and the commanding officer at once made requisition for 20,000 rounds of 69-caliber to the chief of ordnance. . . . July 30th notice was received from the St. Louis arsenal that ammunition would be shipped, but none reached the post before the attack. Fortunately there were on hand several cases of canister for the 12-pounder howitzers, which contained round balls of caliber 69; these were used for the muskets, the powder for the cartridges being obtained from the treaty train. The canisters were filled with broken pieces of cast iron and other materials. In this way about 2000 cartridges were provided.

September 4th and 5th frequent shots were fired from across the river. About daybreak on the 6th the Indians attacked the post with increased force. They succeeded in getting into the stable, where a sharp fight took place for about ten minutes. Two Indians were killed and many wounded, and two of our men slightly wounded. After being driven from the stable the Indians attacked the fort from three sides, south, east, and north. The hottest of the contest was at the commissary buildings, and at this point the howitzer did very effective service, as was shown by the fact that the Indians left their dead upon the battlefield. Eight or ten were found there, half buried in the sand, on the bank of the river. On the west side of the new commissary building there was also a hot contest. Here was a small breast-work of hewed logs, defended by about 10 privates under Sergeants William Deutch and Fred Simon. This small force fought nobly, though greatly out-numbered, and succeeded in killing and wounding many braves. Two of the killed were within thirty or forty feet of the breastworks. The Indians failed to penetrate the garrison at these two points, concentrated their force at the southeast corner near the stables and the ferry. Here the fight, at times most furious, lasted until 3 P.M., the Indians losing many warriors. The post interpreter, Joseph Demarais (a half-breed), subsequently learned from the attacking force that their losses were so heavy that they were discouraged from renewing the attempt to take the fort. Our loss was one killed, Private Wm. Siegel, and two wounded in the whole day's fight.

From this date there were no further attacks except from small squads of Indians, who would fire at the fort from the opposite side . . . and vigilance was also maintained at Fort Ripley. . . . With scarcely a warning signal, the state was precipitated into all the horrors of an Indian war. . . . The Chippewas in the north were restless and eager to join them. . . . Had these outposts fallen, a horde of barbarians from the north would have made . . . the fairest portions of Minnesota their easy prey. . . .

Captain Emil Burger, Commanding

By the end of November, we'd made good progress in widening and clearing rough spots in the road to Sauk Centre, about fifty miles to the northwest of Forrest City. In addition to the road work, we'd gotten in some drilling and practice in marksmanship. Some of that practice had been on deer, rabbits, and even on the ducks on the lake before it froze. Word came back from Fort Snelling that the Third Regiment had praised our shooting, as well as progress made in building the post.

We received orders to build another post in Sauk Centre. Rumor said that there'd be another one in between, later, on the Sauk River. The series of posts were to be guarded stopover points for the wagon trains supplying posts and forts to the west as far as Fort Abercrombie. Also, Governor Ramsey wanted to build up assurance so that the settlers would feel it was safe to go home and plant crops. The development of the whole frontier had been set back by ten or twenty years by the crazy Indian uprising. That had to be remedied.

77

Troops from most of the western forts were being pulled back to Fort Snelling. Steamboats could supply that fort with wheat and supplies. The western forts had to be supplied by wagons, where before they had depended on buying beef and wheat from the settlers. The garrison at Fort Ridgley had been increased. Coloney Sibley, (soon they began to call him General), was busy arranging the release of the women and children taken captive by the Sioux and in accepting the surrender of penitent warriors who wished they'd stayed on their reservations.

Rumors of the battles at New Ulm and Birch Coolie were confirmed.[10] It was a busy winter for troops in Minnesota.

We failed to finish all that Captain Pettit had planned for Sauk Centre before the snow left and mud came. It had been a wet, "open" winter. By March more than half of Company B had come down sick with heavy colds and lung fevers. We did well to keep a full crew hauling logs and another clearing roads.

In May, the wagon trains got as far west as Sauk Centre and we went along to Alexandria as guard. With warmer weather we were feeling better; nearly everyone was able to be up and working. We'd heard that there'd been trouble with the Chippewas above Fort Ripley, on the Mississippi. Part of our job was to make a big show of strength to cheer the settlers. Lieutenant Hollister took forty men to guard a train of twenty-five wagons. Lieutenant Shaw followed, guarding a bigger one. Forty men on the march can look like a lot of rifles. We were cheered with a whoop by people on the street in Alexandria.

I liked the marching. It gave Frank and me a chance to put the men through some skirmish formations as well as close order drill. After most of the men in our platoons were over the spell of colds and fever, we began to pick up. By May, many of us were in better condition than during the previous summer. Even Frank got over the chest cold he'd had ever since Christmas. Working in the timber had built us up. God knows we needed the relief from colds, and the healthy outdoor exercise.

The Punitive Expedition Against The Sioux In 1863

Sauk Centre — May 11th, 1863[11]

Dear Wife:

I once more take my pen in hand to write to you a line knowing that you are anxious to hear often . . . the Paymaster was here on the 9th of this month and payed us two months wages. I got ten dollars more than was due me on the other payment and it was taken out of this so it left me but twenty-four dollars. I don't know how much I can send home yet or how I can send it. . . . I was in hopes to have got more money to send you but I can't help it. . . . It is eleven o'clock and I must stop and go on my guard duty.

I waited until the mail came in to get a letter from you but got none and I feel rather down about it. . . . God bless you.

B. F. Pierce

We all enjoyed those trips to Alexandria. There was one lake where we always managed to camp that had bass so hungry we could catch them with a bit of yarn or a feather for bait. After a march of thirty miles, plus all the open order drill we put the men through on the march, bass tasted plenty good.

On our second trip, we went as guards clear to Fort Abercrombie. The trip took more than three weeks. On the way back a special messenger brought us orders to meet Captain Pettit and Company B on the Redwood River, west of Fort Ridgley. General Sibley's orders had assembled almost four thousand men and eight pieces of artillery for a great sweep across the plains. He claimed he'd sweep all the renegade Sioux across the Missouri. The troops were jubilant. Now maybe we'd have a chance to teach the renegade Sioux a lesson.

Our two platoons had only one night of rest on the Redwood River. We had to march extra hours every day to get there in time. Lieutenant Hollister was fore-thoughted enough to send a man on ahead on his own horse, to report our arrival to Captain Pettit and to ask them to cook rations for us.

The first person I recognized as we climbed the bank of Redwood River was Sergeant Jones. But now he was wearing the double bars of a captain. The whoop he gave when he saw us may not have been becoming to the dignity of an officer, but it made us feel that we were welcome.

"Mighty good to see you, Sergeant Morgan. You're just the man I need to handle a gun crew. Most of my old squad were needed at Fort Ridgley. I've got all green crews, except for Sergeant Callahan, here. Remember him?

80

He was only a corporal when we fought those battles together."

"Of course I remember you, Callahan. We were on the six-pounder together. Then you took over."

"We've got that same gun with us on this trip. It's the best of the lot. I sure hope you'll join us."

"I'll have to see what Captain Pettit's orders are. But it would be nice to ride a mule again. Just now I'm tired of walking. We've come thirty miles since daybreak."

"And you may have a long day tomorrow. General Sibley's orders are to break camp at daylight and take marching formation. We may not go more than a dozen miles but it'll be a wild day. We made only four miles on the day we left Fort Ridgley. Half the men couldn't find their ration wagons and went to bed hungry. I hope we're better organized by now. They've made several changes in company officers."

"Where'd all these new men come from?"

"Several hundred of them are settlers who couldn't go back to their farms. We got a big contingent of settlers from northern Iowa — after the Spirit Lake massacre. The rest were assembled from men of the Fifth and Seventh, and from Renville Rangers."

"This ought to be a rip-roaring campaign with nothing barred. The settlers will all have plenty reason to hate the Sioux. All the Indians we saw up along the Red River of the North were Chippewas. They weren't very warlike. They were just heading west, hoping to take over some of the hunting grounds abandoned by the Santees and Yanktonais we are after."

My squad had been hiking in broken ranks as we followed Captain Jones toward the northwestern section of the huge camp. Presently I saw Sergeant Calvin waving at us from the top of a small ridge beyond a row of tents of the Renville Rangers.

"Where's your camp?" I yelled. He jerked his thumb behind him and waved again as Frank called a greeting.

81

"Glad you got here. Follow that trail on ahead, turn to the right, and you'll be in camp." He waved again and disappeared beyond a hazel bush and some sumac. I stopped my platoon.

"Let's go into camp like soldiers, men. Make it brisk and keep your lines dressed to the right. Now, 'Fall in by fours. Dress your lines. For'd march!' " Sergeant Pierce's platoon fell in behind mine, and his bull-voiced orders brought a dozen heads over the bush tops as arms waved a welcome.

When we neared Captain Pettit's tent I wheeled my platoon into line and saluted the Captain. "Second Platoon, Company B, reporting all present, sir."

And right behind us Frank's voice in a subdued bellow reported his detachment from the Fourth Platoon.

"Where's Lieutenant Hollister?"

"He stopped at the corrals to tend to his horse, sir. Here is his written report. He'll be along in a few minutes."

The Captain dismissed us with a warning to eat hearty. Any breakfast might be hurried and skimpy. I was almost too tired to eat, but the smell of boiling stew and hot coffee helped all of us to relax and put away a good meal. Knots of men were eagerly elaborating on all they'd done in the past three weeks. I took my cup of coffee over to where Captain Pettit was talking with Captain Jones.

"Pull up a box and sit, Sergeant. Captain Jones says that he needs you to drill a gun crew. How'd you like that?"

"Right well, Captain, if you can put me on detached duty."

"Only temporarily, Sergeant. But training gun crews is important. We'll need experienced gunners if we meet any sizeable bunch of renegades. I want to compliment you and Sergeant Pierce on the way your men are handled. They've shaped up into a well drilled squad. And every man looks fit. Has any of them learned enough about a rifle to outshoot Sergeant Pierce?"

"No. And I doubt if any ever will. He shoots deer so far away that we've asked him to just shoot the ones on ahead in the line of march, so we don't have to carry 'em so far. He rarely shoots more than once. Jerusha! What a rifle he has!"

"Better than your Henry?"

"He shoots either one better than any of us. With him and his squad in the supporting line, I'd never worry a minute about an Indian charge getting close to our artillery."

Captain Jones said, "I noticed that most of his men shoot better than average. He must be a good teacher."

"He says a good shot doesn't eat any more than a poor shot. It's better to have a dozen experts with a rifle than a whole platoon of men who can't hit what they're shooting at."

I listened to some more of their casual comments as long as I could stand it and then blurted out, "Any mail for me, sir?"

Captain Pettit grinned broadly as he pulled two letters out of his dispatch case. "I saved them for you, Sergeant. My, they smell nice," and his grin broadened to become a belly laugh at my red face. "Glad you've got a girl back home, son. Maybe that will make you take care of yourself in the Indian country. We hope all of you will be coming back, when it's over.

"Your conduct at Fort Ridgley and that of Sergeant Pierce was mentioned in dispatches to General Sibley. You will soon be promoted to the permanent grade of First Sergeant — you've earned it by doing the work and taking the responsibility all winter. I expect you'll be a lieutenant when we come back. I like to see a man of your ability and education get ahead."

I was flabbergasted. I'd never had the dash and leading ability of men like Frank Pierce. Nor his skill with a rifle, nor in teaching our men to use one. We'd fought hard at Fort Ridgley because it had been do or die. If the savages had broken our line we'd all have been massacred. I'd enjoyed working the twelve-pounder. I looked down and found that I'd bent my letters all out of shape. So I changed the subject.

"When can I start helping to train gun crews, sir? I'd like that since I have your permission."

"Tomorrow. I'll give you written orders for detached duty. On this campaign our Company B will usually be assigned to give support and protection to the artillery. Men fight best when they're supported by friends. You'll still have the responsibility for your Second Platoon — rations and supplies. Now you'd better get some sleep. We'll have a hectic day tomorrow until our line of march is organized."

But it was hard to get to sleep that night. Several men from our platoons were sitting around our campfire swapping tall stories with other men. I kept thinking about the friendly letters I'd gotten from Susan. I decided not to show them to Frank until later. He hadn't gotten any word from Carrie. I wanted to let the misery die out of his eyes before he saw my mail. I just don't understand wives.

The next thing I knew, it was beginning to get light and I heard men stirring. Cooking fires began to light up the ridge near us. I put on my boots and roused our detail for getting breakfast. Then I walked over to the break in the ridge and looked down toward the river. Cooking fires began to flicker like fireflies in the dark hollow. A thin film of fog drifted toward me from the river. Men were stumbling down between the tents to get drinking and washing water before the horseboys led their lines of horses and mules down to the river to drink.

The sky in the east was beginning to turn the coppery pink that presaged a hot humid day. The waning moon hung in the darker sky above the western horizon. Wrens flitted into a bush and a thrush ran from one bush to another with a rustling sound as it kicked its way through

84

the dry leaves looking for insects. It was the busy time for birds.

Downstream and near the river a bugle called the camp awake. Across the hollow a mule brayed his dissatisfaction with army life and I heard the rattle of bars in the corral gate. Because this was close to home and the camp had been there a week, they'd built a corral. On the march they'd picket the stock where there was grass. Horses were harder to guard than mules from Indian attack but mules were stouter under the pack saddle or in harness, and more hardy.

In the few minutes I'd been listening and watching, the camp had come fully awake. There was the calling of orders and the laughter of joking men. Frank's voice rolled across the ridge calling for a corporal's detail to attend to the Captain's horse. I hurried back to detail some men to go with me while I drew the day's rations. Frank sent along his own corporal. We often trusted each other to draw all our rations. Frank never cheated. Some of the sergeants were not as dependable. They'd keep the biggest and best of everything.

By the time we got back with rations, the cooks were ladling out oatmeal mush sprinkled with a smidgin of brown sugar. Back home we'd have had cream or milk with it. In the army we'd learned to do without. On most of that campaign we lived on mush in the morning, hard bread and fresh meat for noon dinner — if we were given time to cook it — and hard bread with stew for supper. There were no fresh fruits or vegetables, not even old potatoes. Apparently we were expected to live off the deer, buffalo, and antelope we could kill.

This was called a "punitive expedition," to wreck vengeance on all the renegade Indians who had been with Little Crow, but hadn't surrendered in the fall of 1862. We were to move fast and search them out. Nearly fifty half-breeds went with us to identify any chiefs who had engaged in the massacre and bring them back for trial.

85

Those who felt any regrets for their part in the murders and rapes had already surrendered.[12]

As we marched west we learned to appreciate how General Sibley planned his march. He wisely rotated, among the various companies, the honor — and danger — of leading the line of march. He favored those companies who maintained the best discipline. By giving them the responsibility of scouting ahead of the line of march they could also shoot deer, buffalo, or antelope to keep the brigade supplied with meat. The scouts would mark the killed game with a flag or cloth on a pole and go on with their duty. Men from the commissary would dress out the meat and pack it in. Providing meat for four thousand men took a lot of hunting. But game, or the lack of it, gave a clue to the presence of Indians in the area.

One advantage in leading the line of march was the chance to pick the best game for the use of one's own company and the headquarters' staff. Also, the leaders had first choice in camping spots after the General had chosen the place to camp. And that competition for the honor of leading the column made for efficiency in duty among the men. It was also the cause of some jealousy among the officers, especially the young West Pointers who had been assigned to raw recruits. Our artillery usually were ordered well up toward the front and got no worse than second choice, since our guns guarded the van.

The worst place in the column was at rear guard. In dry weather those men got the full benefit of dust as the wagons wallowed along. In wet weather it was the rear guard who had to assist with back and shoulder when the wagons got stuck in mucky creeks and vales. And the rear guard had no lack of danger. On other campaigns (in Nebraska) the most successful raids by the Indians had been sudden forays on the wagon train to get guns, powder, and supplies, then a gallop out of musket range.

And when there was an emigrant train with women, as on our campaign, the rear guard had to be alert to our own soldiers as well as renegade Indians. Guarding the rear was certain to be dirty. In this campaign it was often given to good but unfortunate officers who had been saddled with companies of incompetent, sour men.

On the morning we left Redwood River there was much confusion and little progress. Staff couriers raced madly from General Sibley's tent on the highest ridge, ordering and imploring the various companies to take their correct place in the line of march. Invariably, as the dust would settle around a company already in place, some other company would try to get around it and go ahead. Another courier would race away from the General's tent and order them back into line. The General had been a judge in the Territorial Government before he became the first Governor of Minnesota and had been noted for firmness rather than good nature. By the middle of the afternoon he had lost his voice. New orders and reprimands had to be written out. It was a hard day for all of us.

Captain Pettit had trained Company B to obey orders in a hurry. But even he lost his temper when one company after another of the Iowa troops tried to crowd in ahead.

"Where's your captain?" he demanded of one dapper trooper in a brand new cap and sergeant's stripes. "You're supposed to take station two companies behind us. Can you read orders?"

"What's the difference who is first? We damn well can't wait all day for you deadheads to decide to march."

"You'll follow orders in this army or I'll bet General Sibley finds some new officers. And I'll do my best to see that you're never one of them." Captain Pettit was white with anger at the man's insolence to an officer.

The man's profane reply was cut short by the arrival of an angry captain who had been roundly chewed out by a courier from Headquarters. "Get your platoons back into their proper place or I'll break every sergeant in the company," he yelled. "I'll put you men through some drill that'll teach you it's worth while to obey orders," and for

87

thirty minutes he sat his horse and gave them close order drill, yelling like a first sergeant. His language was not much credit to West Point.

"Those Iowa companies didn't want to come up here in the first place," Lieutenant Hollister told me. "General Sibley has already replaced two of their elected captains with army men. There'll be some hard feelings before the men find out that their new officers are boss. Volunteers can be as undependable as a flock of hens. We're lucky to have the kind of men that enlisted in Company B — and the sergeants we got."

In the dispatches and orders sent to Captain Pettit that night was one that he read to us as we stood at attention in front of our tents. It was a note from General Sibley: "To the Officers and men of Company B, Ninth Regiment: It is with pleasure that I compliment all of you in maintaining line of march and on the dispatch with which you followed orders. Army Regulars could not have done better." Captain Pettit added, "That is high praise from the General. I am proud of you."

It was nice to know that the General remembered to praise as well as censure, but a chewing out came more frequently.

In spite of the confused start and the "hurry up — and wait" that went on all day, we camped that night more than ten miles from the old camp on Redwood River. Some of the units didn't arrive until after dark — even later than the wagon train carrying our rations and supplies. One of the tardy companies was made up of the ninety-day recruits who had tried to crowd in ahead of us. From the ridge where we camped we could hear their newly appointed captain bawling orders as he marched them by column of fours to a spot near the mules of the supply train. His orders came sharp and clear but the men looked completely worn out and subdued. A courier from Headquarters was waiting for them. He was not smiling as he saluted and handed the Captain a folded paper. The Captain saluted without any comment.

88

"I'll bet they get rear guard duty tomorrow," Frank said to me. "And I'll bet we get to lead the column one of these days if we can continue to keep our men in line. The hard part of maintaining discipline will come when we get to the antelope country and the men get the itch to hunt a little."

"And I expect you're the one who'll itch the worst. You used to bring in more game than anyone else."

"Four thousand men will need a lot of meat," he said and grinned. "I wouldn't want anyone to go hungry."

In the next two weeks Frank's platoon got its full share of leading the column. As scouts, they sent in loads of deer, antelope, and presently buffalo to keep the brigade well supplied with fresh meat. They almost made up for the scouts who didn't find — or couldn't shoot — any game. Whenever possible Frank and two or three of his men would scout ahead in the early morning and kill game close to the line of march. His skill and planning always pleased General Sibley.

Considering that the General was not a professional soldier and that he had several West Point officers under his command, there was splendid morale among both officers and men. His marching orders made sense to me. I liked being near the lead with the artillery. But to the careless and antagonistic men who generally drew rear guard duty it was a summer of dust, or mud and wet work, helping the supply wagons along. Most of them continued to be in trouble.

We had good reason to believe that there were Indians in front and on both sides of us. Our scouts rarely saw them — only where they'd been. Bands of cavalry came in to report.

"Where did that squadron of cavalry come from?" I asked Frank one day. "I never saw them before."

"They're some of General Sully's men. He's south of the Missouri River, sweeping west same as we are, trying to push all the Sioux on ahead. The cavalry is supposed to keep both brigades in touch. All this hunting and shooting has helped to keep the little bands bunching up for protection. The warfare between tribes and smaller groups has been forgotten for the summer. They're all against *us*."

"If we can catch 'em?"

"If they gather enough warriors they'll give us a battle. Our best hope is to crowd them so close they can't get their families and supplies across the Missouri ahead of us. We may be able to hurt 'em bad enough so they'll be glad to stay on their reservations. We've *got* to win this campaign. If we don't, the pioneer settlements won't be safe for a dozen years. It isn't just our settlers. The Sioux will be marauding all over Iowa, Nebraska, and Kansas, too. If it ever comes to that, we'll find we're in a war of extermination."

"Where is General Sully?"

"I heard General Sibley say that he's coming up the Missouri in boats. He should be on ahead of us. But part of his brigade is escorting two hundred wagons of supplies for the western forts. He's supposed to meet us at the big bend of the Missouri."

"I keep wondering why we have such a big train of army wagons." Captain Pettit had joined us and I looked toward him, "We're wearing out wagons and mules faster'n we're eating bread."

"We have orders to establish several new posts — and a fort on the James River and one on the Missouri. On the trip back to Fort Ridgley we'll travel light."

"Then this will be sort of a holding action, with a line of forts? The Sioux will just slip on by us."

"We mostly want to push them west. When the Sioux come east it always means trouble. In other years they raided the Winnebagoes. For the past year the chiefs who have been in favor of war have been telling the others that we're too busy fighting the southern rebels to defend the western settlements. This is their chance to kill settlers and drive us east of the Mississippi. If we don't punish

90

the renegades who were with Little Crow their next attack will be on the mining camps, and our whole western territory will be in ruins."

Sergeant Calvin spoke up, "I think the only good Indian is a dead one. They're all murderers."

"The Indians who are willing to stay on reservations and accept the annuity beef and money to help out their hunting are not much trouble. The war bands are *all* bad. It's that simple. We'll try to kill or capture any Indian found off his reservation."

That was the way most of us felt about it. It was easy to separate the peaceful Indians from the renegades. Most of us had seen the burned cabins of the settlers. Some of us had lost loved ones in the massacres in Minnesota. None who had seen the dead bodies in 1862 would have any qualms in killing a warrior off the reservation — and we weren't near any reservations. And there weren't any between us and the Missouri River.

The march across the Dakota prairie soon settled into a steady routine of hard work. The line of march took shape by four o'clock in the morning. The day's march ended about twelve hours later, depending on where General Sibley decided on a suitable camping and grazing area. Some horses and mules will graze at night but reasonable care of our stock required a period of daylight grazing also. By the rules laid down for the march, the head of the line went into camp downstream on whatever river or creek we'd come to. They filled their canteens and cooking pots before the stock were led to water. As other companies arrived they took position upstream in turn, where the water was still clear. Sometimes the men got in a hurry and muddied the water before those downstream could fill their canteens, but there was surprisingly little trouble of that kind in the 1863 campaign.

Usually we sergeants detailed a pair of men to cut wood or to gather buffalo chips and build a fire. Another pair put up the tents, and others unsaddled the horses and

91

attached lines to let them graze. Another detail drew supplies and cooked supper. Evening made a welcome break to the monotony of marching. Camp chores kept us busy till dark.

Meanwhile General Sibley would send out his orders for the line of march for the following day. The cavalry usually camped on the flanks of the supply wagons and the emigrant train, both for protection against Indian attack and to find grazing for their horses. The General's staff camped near the upstream end of camp, and the artillery camped nearby, so it fell to our lot to take care of the officers' horses.

Before daylight the men detailed to help the horseboys bring in and saddle or harness the horses and mules had been routed out. Putting on their boots brought loud groans of agony as they yawned and hurried to their tasks a jump ahead of the swinging feet of the sergeants. Companies detailed to lead the line of march, slurped their cups of coffee and hurried on. A few of their men remained to pull down their tents, pack the blankets and cooking pots and heave everything aboard the supply wagons as they came by.

Meanwhile, Captain Jones had detailed which guns were to support the van and those that were to fall in with the wagons. Both groups had to catch their mules and hitch them to the guns, amid the confusion of scores of other objecting mules and men. Squadrons of cavalry formed on the flanks of the line of march while the mules and oxen for the wagons were harnessed and hitched up. There was a standing rule that the oxen were to be on the march ahead of the rest because they were slower. In spite of orders and vigorous swearing, they were seldom ready in time and invariably slowed our march — or at least the rear guard all day.

By daylight the mounted infantry had packed their equipment, found their ponies and saddled them, ate breakfast, filled their canteens and fell into line to protect the supply wagons and emigrant train as required. By five o'clock the wagons and mounted men covered an area a quarter of a mile wide and a mile long. And by then the harsh shouts of the rear guard were pushing the stragglers, both men and animals, to move up.

Part of the duty of the scouts was to choose the best route of march. Even when following old tracks, it was not easy. Bogs became almost impassible after a rain, and wagons ahead had churned them into mire hub deep. Alternate routes often ended in rocks or steep-banked gullies. Obstructions pinched in the sides of the column and accidents usually left a wagon blocking the most needed routes. Certain drivers had more than their share of getting bogged down, tipping over, or breaking a wheel. The emigrant train was even less disciplined — and more demanding. The walking infantry were called upon to help almost every day for at least an hour of lifting and pulling. Yet we were averaging more than twenty miles a day.

All of the line was noisy. Mules seemed to respond only to angry words. Oxen required frequent prodding, and a curse added vigor to the prod and also aroused the attention of the oxen. Four thousand men clutter up a lot of country.

There was some friction. We had our share of misfits or the lazy, inept, stubborn, selfish, and mean-tempered. But the misfits drew more of the detail of dust and mud with the rear guard. Captain Pettit and Company B got more scouting and detail for supporting our artillery near the van. I must admit that General Sibley favored us — and I think we earned it. Our discipline and efficiency were well above average.

On the 4th of July we reached the big bend of the Cheyenne River. We were too busy and tired to celebrate the day, except that it was notable for the big dinner that night. Frank shot six buffalo in the forenoon, and my squad helped to bring in the youngest cow to make sure there

93

were tenderloin steaks for Company B. Lieutenant Shaw had worked as a butcher and taught us to cut meat so it would be as tender as possible.

When Frank pointed it out he said, "Leave the big bull for the cavalry. They can't miss it. It'll be tough as rawhide and they're always bragging about how tough *they* are."

From our camp that night we could see trees along the Cheyenne River. One of the older scouts told us to take a good look at the timber. "You'll see precious few trees from here to the breaks of the Missouri. Just grass and buffalo."

As we slanted up a ridge next morning, the land stretched out in endless prairie. There didn't seem to be a thing for an Indian to hide behind. I sighed at the peacefulness.

Frank must have read my thoughts. "Warn everyone on patrol to watch extra carefully. Don't let the open space fool you. There may be a dozen swales between here and the horizon — and some of them filled with warriors. I've glimpsed their scouts off to the south. A big or little band of 'em are riding parallel to us right now."

Captain Pettit kept us in open skirmish formation, with mounted guides to right and left. About four o'clock General Sibley rode forward looking for a place to camp.

"Your scouts haven't shot any game today, Captain. What are they so busy about that they forgot to hunt?"

"We've been watching for game but since there hasn't been any I expect we're following a band of Indians. I know there are some not far to the south."

"Looks like some of your men have found something, now."

I'd been watching where two of our men had disappeared in a fold of the prairie. After more than five minutes one of them reappeared and waved us on. When I got there the scouts were showing the General and Captain Pettit a freshly beaten trail. The buckskin pony I'd been issued was no match for the Captain's chestnut or the General's big black jumper.

94

Our lead scout, Tim Cully, was saying, "These horses were running hard. Looks like there had been an ambush."

Following the trail, we came onto the remains of a horse partially eaten by wolves. "Must have been more than twenty horses in this bunch," Cully went on, reading sign. "I expect we'll find where the ambushers were hiding in that gully. Yep, here's where they were grazing their horses."

The sign was plain as he read it. The grazing must have lasted for more than an hour. We could see where the men had lain at the edge of the gully. Cully went over the area very carefully. He picked up a few empty cartridges.

"At least two of the attackers had breech-loaders, sir, and here's the mark made by an old trade musket."

Tim Cully said that the dead pony looked like the shaggy horses used by the Minnetonkas and Chippewas up around Fort Abercrombie. Several others agreed with him.

"Looks like the northern tribes are already hunting this far west. I wonder if they're helping us — or hunting us?"

"Any idea where the ambushing party might have come from?" General Sibley wanted to know. He had given orders to one of his staff to halt the column and to set up camp down by a bigger creek than this trickle. An Indian interpreter had come over and was looking on.

Cully held up a bit of buffalo hide obviously stepped on by a horse and torn from a pouch. He showed it to the Indian. "Cured in a hurry with salt? Yanktonais?"

The Indian nodded. "Maybe cured on a hunting trip in the sun. Not cured with smoke by squaw. Maybe Sissipapa."

General Sibley listened carefully. Up to now the Indians and half-breeds with us had been of little use. It seemed significant to me that the General depended on our own men for scouting and never allowed the interpreters any guns better than a musket. Now he asked, "What does the ambush mean?"

"Chippewas are out here again, hunting. They were driven out of the high prairie by the Dakotas last summer. They are back. Now the Sioux are waylaying them, hoping

95

to catch their horses and get a few scalps as well as their guns."

"These Sioux seem to have better rifles than we can get. Where do they come from?"

The interpreter shrugged, "Maybe traders up north."

General Sibley looked at each empty shell. "Last winter I wrote to General (John) Pope that Canadian traders were supplying the Sioux with better guns than we were getting for our troops. That trading has got to be stopped — somehow. I'm glad you noticed these shells. I'll issue orders for anyone seeing Indian tracks to watch for spent shells and to bring them to me. I want proof about these traders. And some Americans have been trading with the Sioux, selling them rifles and stirring them up to take advantage of the Rebellion. It has to stop!

"Sergeant Morgan, I expect Captain Jones is eager for you to put one of the gun crews through an hour's drill. He says that you have been a big help to him. Your extra hours, training his crews, are paying off. I appreciate it. We're going to need artillery support mighty soon now. I've mentioned your extra work in dispatches. You're due for promotion."

I saluted and hurried over to where Captain Jones was already drilling one crew on a six-pounder. My detached duty with him was already helping me. I could turn my horse over to one of my scouts and be relieved of guard duty and other chores. I joined Sergeant Williams, who led the crew on another gun. We gave the men an hour of fast drill. This constant practice was cutting down their loading time to a dependable minimum. By a steady count I was able to know exactly how long to cut a fuse, load the shell, and fire it out over the enemy. With practice we'd be able to lay our shells where they'd do the most damage.

Captain Jones had already emplaced his guns where they commanded any approach from the south or west. As we finished our drill, spatters of rain warned us of the thundershower we had expected all afternoon. We whipped

96

on gun covers and put tarps over the caissons. Men all over camp hurried with tents. I dashed with Sergeant Williams into his tent which was nearer than my own. He urged me to sit down and relax.

"The men all appreciate what you've shown us, Sergeant Morgan. That's why they're willing to do their extra work, too. You're doing two jobs."

"I'm just trying to get us ready for any savages we fight. This extra practice may save our lives."

Captain Jones stuck his head in the tent flap. "May I come in?" he asked. "I'm soaked. Right after the shower began I saw that the knot-headed mule-skinners had left the tarp off of one of the supply wagons loaded with cased guns. I had to spend fifteen minutes routing them out of a tent to cover it."

"That's the commissary for you. We've already found out they're short of salt. They only sent the same amount we'd have needed if they'd sent along salt beef in kegs."

Captain Jones nodded agreement. "I wish you could spend more time with me, Morgan. Your help has given me more time for reports and filling out forms. But I need still more help. You could do a lot of it if you were in my command. The red tape takes too much time. I see Captain Pettit and other captains sitting up all hours writing reports and keeping accounts. It is beginning to wear them down. This is the longest spell of forced marching I've seen in ten years of service. If I could get you and Frank Pierce transferred to the artillery, I'd get you your commissions as lieutenants."

"Captain Pettit has already requested a commission for Frank Pierce, sir. His squad of expert riflemen has caught the eye of General Sibley. And he deserves it. He's taught them to be the best riflemen in the brigade.

"And the way Corporal Tim Cully read sign today really impressed the General. He was sharp enough to know the importance of those empty cartridges. Knowing the Sioux have new rifles will let us be ready for 'em."

97

"Tim is a sharp boy, Morgan. And Pierce was wise to get him promoted to corporal. I'm proud of the way your Company B and my artillerymen are shaping up. Sergeant Williams, I noticed that your men have been getting your howitzer into position and loaded faster than Lieutenant Whipple's crew. He noticed it, too. It all helps to get his men to try harder. But learn from him in sighting his gun. He's good. In any major action against the Indians we may have to operate as three, or more, separate artillery units, either to fight off a charge from all sides or to catch them in a cross-fire. You're doing fine."

"Thanks, Captain. And I appreciate your showing me how to judge fuse time and how to explode canister to advantage. I'm getting eager to see how our men work under fire."

" 'Sufficient unto the day is the evil thereof,' " he quoted.

Jones was a little man, black-haired, and with a wide black beard that hid the fact that the top hooks on his tunic were always unfastened. He was a bundle of energy, deep-voiced and strong, and as durable as our mules for all his pint size. His men affectionately called him "Twenty-two short," because of the little Sharps .22 pepperbox pistol that he carried. Some of them laughed at it, but I felt pretty sure he'd shoot out the eyeball of any Indian who got within spear range of the cannon Jones was working.

I'd seen Captain Jones handle shells with an ease that was unbelievable in a man of his light weight. He knew exactly where each gun in our battery of eight guns would drop its shells. For instance, the howitzer I worked with Sergeant Williams always shot high and to the left. For that reason I cut the fuse for it a bit shorter than for other guns in firing spherical case shells. Jones' sense of timing was remarkable, and his equipment was spotless, placed ready for use each night, and with everything carefully covered against dew or rain.

I'd never heard him swear, although he'd get so annoyed that the cords would stand out on his neck like red ropes.

98

But whenever he had to jump in and do someone's work in the way it should be done, and then would turn and walk away without a word, that man was careful not to be slack in his job again. In the three campaigns on which I was with him, I never saw him alarmed during a battle. He never showed any fear of bullets, mules, or Indians. But when we were drilling with the guns, he wanted everything done by count, with no slipups or any slack work.

"Captain Jones burns with a mighty short fuse," one of his fellow captains had commented early in the campaign. "I hope he never explodes near me."

A new shower began just as we were eating supper. In two minutes my pannikin of stew was half water. In an hour the campsite was a sea of mud. Over beyond the artillery park, the horses and mules in their rope corral stood with heads hanging almost to the ground, their wet sides glinting in the occasional gleams from the cooking fires, kept burning so that men coming in from picket duty could partially dry out before crawling under damp blankets. It still lacked an hour of sunset, but the clouds pressed so low that it was almost as dark as night. Extra patrols had been detailed for duty. All of them had orders to keep in touch with each other at intervals.

This was the kind of night that Indians picked for sneaking up on a sentry — and he might not be found until morning. It was unusual for a picket to see an Indian close enough to challenge him or exchange shots. But we knew that we were getting close to the main ingathering of the Sioux. Twice we had come onto camps less than a week old. They still stunk, and we had to detour to avoid the filth they'd left.

On the 17th of July we were overtaken by a company of scouts from General Sully's brigade with dispatches. The Sioux were hurrying southwest ahead of us. Two items of news soon made the rounds of our camp. Henry H. Sibley had been confirmed as Brigadier General, by orders of General John Pope. Most of us were pleased. Captain Pettit hurried over to say so.

99

The second bit of news located the main Sioux camp of several thousand lodges about fifty miles away, between us and the Missouri River. Also that day we were visited by a group of nearly three hundred half-breed Indians. A robed Jesuit priest rode into camp with their leaders. He gave his name as Father Andre. They claimed to be friendly and they were hungry. No game had been seen in the past three days.

"What can they expect?" I asked Frank. "They've been following us. Our four thousand men have probably scared all the game away from our trail for ten miles."

We had plenty of meat and fed them well. I heard General Sibley advising Father Andre to lead them north into better hunting. They offered to fight with us if we'd give them guns. But the General must have seen the look in Father Andre's eye for he shook his head and explained that we had no extra guns.

Also, I wondered what use it would be to give them guns? Most of those they had were rusty and nearly useless. I never knew an Indian to keep his gun clean and oiled. Half-breeds are almost as bad. I pointed out one to Frank, who had come over to where I'd been talking with Captain Jones. "Look at that musket! It might have been a fine gun at one time. Now I wonder if it will even shoot?"

"It might — or blow up in his face. The barrel is full of dirt and rust. The rear sight's been broken off. It's just an iron club."

It rained the next day, and the next. We'd dug shallow trenches and low earthworks at some of our encampments. Here at Camp Atchison we dug deep trenches. For two days we worked in rain and mud to enlarge old trenches and dig new ones to make a system of defense, enclosing a large spring and about an acre of meadow sloping up to a ridge.

There was considerable speculation about these defenses. Some of the men declared that we were about to be attacked by at least five thousand savages. Then the real reason came out. We were to leave most of the supply wagons here, to be picked up on the way back to Minnesota. The emigrant train, headed for Fort Benton on the upper Missouri, would push on with a small escort, being pretty sure that our brigade was sweeping the Sioux warriors on southwest to the Missouri, and away from the northern trail to Fort Benton.

About two-thirds of our brigade, traveling light, were to press on and try to overtake the Sioux before they could get across the Missouri and into the badlands to the southwest.

On the 21st we marched over twenty-five miles to Camp Olin. On the next day we crossed the James River after having marched forty-eight miles in two days. Two days later we overtook a large body of Indians near Big Mound. Forward scouts had been reporting them since noon. About one o'clock, one of our half-breed interpreters was sent forward to where Sergeant Calvin and some scouts were clustered, at a distance of a long musket-shot from a similar group of Indians on ponies. They were in full battle regalia. One scout came riding back to tell General Sibley that these were Red Cloud's men, a relative of our half-breed interpreter, and one of the most peaceable of the Sissipapa chiefs.

We had already corralled the wagon train on the shore of a little lake at the first alarm. Men under Colonel Crooks had been set to digging entrenchments along two ridges ahead of the mule corral. Indians by the score began to appear on all the hills around us.

Captain Jones called me over to direct the fire of the howitzer under Sergeant Williams. He sent a howitzer with Lieutenant Whipple to support two companies of the Fifth Regiment under Colonel McPhail, who were moving forward ahead of the General's staff. Somehow the peaceful confab between our interpreter and the Indians in feathered headdresses broke into shouts and thrown spears. Our surgeon, Doctor Weiser, was shot dead by a young buck and all hell broke loose. Colonel McPhail was sent forward to where Doctor Weiser had been killed and Lieutenant Whipple galloped up with his howitzer. All the scouts had fired immediately at the Indian who had killed him, but the savage galloped away. Indians by the hundred raced in from the surrounding ridges. After firing one ragged volley, they dropped back into gullies or over a ridge. From an opposite ridge General Sibley was directing Whipple in shelling those gullies with canister.

As Sergeant Williams drove our gun up the main ridge behind Colonel McPhail, a new wave of Indians broke over the top toward us. In a headon charge we would have been wiped out. They outnumbered us six or eight to one. We had barely time enough to swing our gun to the front, on top of a little hill, before the Indians were within musket range. Bullets whistled overhead and whanged into rocks beside us. At least one spanged off the barrel of the howitzer as I was laying it for my first shot with canister. I didn't wait for the blast before I began counting for the reload. As I looked up after the next shot, I saw I must lower the breech. The Indians had turned and were racing for a gully.

Frank Pierce was waving for his men to "Come on." Captain Pettit was waving his shiny, unbloodied sword, trying to follow the maze of ridges on his horse. Pierce's men had dismounted and were climbing up gullies along the animal trails. Now that I had a clear shot, I swung to lead a cluster of Indians hiding in a gully. My shell burst above the Indians, sweeping horses and riders up the gully, or down in sodden heaps. Our riflemen took care of those who waited.

I had no time to watch. Again we hauled our gun up the little ridge. This time we gained the head of the farther gully and fired an explosive shell into it. On the opposite ridge I could see Whipple firing into an angle of the same gully. Indians were scrambling up the sides of the ravine and over the ridge. We had only a scattered target. Frank and his men were closer. Frank dropped to one knee and fired methodically. At every shot an Indian jumped or rolled down the slope. Some of them lay still where they stopped rolling.

Higher up the main ridge, Colonel McPhail was waving his sword and urging his men to follow. He was within musket-shot of the rearmost Indians there. We hauled our howitzer to the top of our own ridge. Suddenly we were facing more than a thousand savages on a new ridge. McPhail's three companies of the Fifth had been joined by a company of the First Minnesota Rangers (Doctor Weiser's own Regiment) and several companies of the men who had been digging trenches (most of us preferred fighting to digging).

As soon as we were within extreme range with the howitzer we began lobbing fragmentary shells across the intervening gullies. On my right, Captain Jones had found a ridge ahead of Lieutenant Whipple. From his forward position he could pepper the Indians with canister. We shelled Indians as long as they were in sight. By then we were blocked by deep gullies.

But it didn't matter. The tail of the warriors were racing away in confusion. Some distance ahead of them we could see moving dots — women, children, dogs, and old men, humped with camp gear and sundry belongings. Our cavalrymen were in hot pursuit, giving the warriors no chance to stand and regroup.

Without specific orders, I felt it best to urge Sergeant Williams to return to camp. I would like to have followed Sergeant Pierce in the pursuit, but I knew that we'd never catch him. I'd been in the front of the line of march since four o'clock that morning. We'd fought and pushed the artillery for more than twenty miles. I'd had nothing to eat since a quick breakfast. Pierce's men were too far ahead to be overtaken.

Also, I was sure that General Sibley would want our gun emplaced to guard the supply train. And there were other reasons. But we had no chance to rest back in camp. Entrenching had been nearly completed to the General's orders, but then he thought of improvements. When a little lake near camp was found to be too alkaline to drink, he ordered the teamsters and a company of Colonel Crooks' men to herd the horses and mules up to two creeks where they could water, and to let them

103

graze until sunset. Meanwhile Captain Pettit had returned with Sergeant Calvin's platoon, and they set up camp for all of us. He complimented me on my work with Sergeant Williams. In the absence of Jones and Whipple, I was put in charge of emplacing the six-pounders and two howitzers.

General Sibley trotted around everywhere, checking defenses and gun emplacements, inspecting the food and urging the men to have a hearty meal. But he looked worried.

I overheard him talking with Colonel Crooks. He'd ordered Colonel McPhail to follow and harass the retreating Indians, but to be back by nightfall, or if that wasn't possible, to bivouac on the prairie. If his courier had found McPhail, the cavalry ought to be returning. But there was no sign of them by dark and a returning scout said our men were still in hot pursuit. With our forces divided like that, we ate supper all standing, so to speak, expecting another attack on the wagon train at any time.

We'd won our first round with the Sioux, but only with a small group of warriors. The teamsters reported short grass and not much water in the streams. Some of the men went down to wash in the lake. They came back with clean clothing, like they'd been washed and rinsed in soapy water, but they still felt sticky after their baths.

Orders came down from General Sibley that we'd move on at daylight to a lake of sweet water a few miles to the southwest. We ate a hurried breakfast and formed a line of march to the new camp near a big pond they called Dead Buffalo Lake.

Just as we came in sight of that sparkling blue water in a hollow filled with tall grass and reeds, we saw the heads of cavalry and mounted infantry coming over the far ridge. In a few minutes they were identified as the Seventh Regiment. With them was most of our Company

B. The Tenth Regiment and McPhail's infantry began to appear next. A few of the mounted men had exhausted infantrymen on behind them. Others were staggering along beside their weary horses, hanging onto stirrup leathers to help pull themselves along. It was hard to tell who were the more exhausted, the men or their horses.

But, worn out as they were, they looked happy. Chasing the Sioux for ten miles had lifted their spirits more than a night of sound sleep. I was riding a mule pulling a gun carriage when they came down the slope. As I came to a little hill opposite the lake shore, Captain Jones rode up and said we had orders to camp beside the lake and rest for the day. It was evident that most of our brigade was too tired to go on. He showed me where to place the gun. Then he made a terse comment. His eyes were hard for once and his lips thin.

"I'd hate to be the courier who took the orders to Colonel McPhail yesterday. Somehow he didn't get it across to the Colonel to return before nightfall. Now we've got an exhausted brigade. We'd be almost helpless if attacked. And there are thousands of Indians working up to an attack. We'll be lucky if our horses are able to go on tomorrow. Two extra hours of pursuing a beaten enemy, and an all-night march back, has lost us a day of pushing the Indian families. We may have to entrench and fight here while the families get away across the Missouri. It will all depend on what the scouts on ahead report."

"Maybe those are some of the scouts, now," and I pointed to several trotting riders coming over a ridge across the pond. "They may have news. At least they keep looking behind them."

As our cavalry began to straggle in, they were ordered to offsaddle and rest their horses, being careful not to let them drink more than a few gulps of water at first, then to graze them on the best grass. The men who had slept at Big Mound hurried to set up this new camp and to dig

105

entrenchments on the nearer ridges. The fortification was hurried from fast to furious when the squadron of scouts raced in from the south and southeast. Another large band of warriors was closing in.

Captain Jones took two six-pounders, not already emplaced to guard the wagons, and advanced to a hill commanding both our edge of the lake and the nearer ridges. One company of pioneers went along to dig quick fortifications for the guns and for the riflemen detailed to support them. Colonel Crooks detailed three companies who had been digging trenches to go forward and support Jones. By then we could all see the reason for the feverish activity. More Indians than we had ever seen appeared on the high ridge across the lake. Apparently they had not noticed the clumps of straggling infantrymen still coming in. They could have cut them off easily.

One large mass of Indians split off and galloped to the west, but we soon saw that it was so they could attack the wagon train from two directions. Possibly they thought our cavalry was still in pursuit of Red Cloud and his retreating warriors. They certainly came in full of confidence now.

General Sibley sent a mounted troop of the Rangers to protect the exhausted stragglers. By the time they had pushed the stragglers together, the first horde of Indians was in a position to outflank our artillery under Captain Jones on the hill south of the wagons. Only a few hundred infantry and two six-pounders stood between the wagons and thousands of Indians. (Captain Jones estimated later that there were at least 1,200 but they looked like more than that to me.)

Lieutenant Whipple's howitzer was closer to the oncoming horde of savages than the six-pounder that Sergeant Williams and I were serving. I think he fired too soon. Some of the leading Indians drew back, but only a few. By the churning of the reeds at the edge of the lake, I could tell that his spherical shell must have exploded short. I fired with the fuse cut to extreme range, cut the next fuse a trifle shorter, and fired again. My second shell exploded just before Whipple's. The churning of horses in the lead of the Indian horde showed that both shells had dropped horses and killed and wounded dozens of riders.

"Where did our first shell explode?" I asked Williams as we loaded again. "I was too busy to look."

"Right there where those two pinto horses are piled up. That slowed the charge a little. Colonel Crooks' riflemen have them in range now. Let's give them another shell in that bunch to the right, Morgan. God, how they come!"

We gave them several. For what seemed like a long time our shelling was barely adequate. The swirling masses of warriors all but overran the far smaller clump of men defending the wagons. By now both Whipple's and our gun were firing into the flank of the Indians. If we'd have been closer we could have used canister to better advantage. As it was, we must have killed more than fifty savages and wounded hundreds.

Scores of the Indian ponies carried second riders or limp bodies across their withers. Then just as I was aiming at a group circling the wagons, they changed direction and headed toward our corralled mules by the lake. A dozen or more of our men had been trying to quiet the frightened mules charging around inside the rope corral. I swung to lead the Indians and fired. This time I watched the spherical shell as it lofted and sank. With unchristian joy I saw the shell burst into an orange-red flower above the leading Indians. Six or eight horses piled up. The others turned and fled with unmanageable haste. Several Indians jumped up to run away on foot and were cut down by the infantrymen among the wagons. A company of Rangers rode in from their flank to spur that retreat into a complete rout. Then the Indian attack was all over.

107

I turned to shake Sergeant William's hand. He was pointing at the fleeing clumps of that once-frightening horde. I'd noticed that Indians could line up for a charge and even hold that line of unified attack until they got excited and the best horses pushed on ahead. Then they were fighting as individuals. I never knew of any who could retreat with any steadiness. But white men could get excited, too. Sergeant Williams was still pointing and his mouth flapped but no words came.

"They look better running away than toward us, don't they," I suggested. "I thought the wagons and then the mules were goners, but they never got close enough to Captain Pettit's riflemen to let them get into the fight. I suppose the whole fight didn't last an hour. But it seemed like all day."

Sergeant Williams started to speak again but all that came out was a big wheezing sigh. I handed him my canteen. He took a big gulp of water and handed it back. I also swallowed a mouthful of the stuff tasting of reeds and frogs and almost gagged. It was worse than the lake water that morning.

"Feeling better?" I asked.

"I'm all right. I just get so excited when they yell like that. They were mostly running away yesterday. I didn't see how we could stop 'em today. There must have been thousands."

"Well, quite a few hundred. We'd better clean up the gun, get the cover on it, and await orders. I expect we'll see more of the beggars. You'll notice that Captain Jones is keeping his men beside the guns up on his hill. And another thing: He's been watching us off and on all the time. Since he didn't send down any special orders, we must have been doing what he wanted. See if he does not congratulate you on your first real fight. He should. We really fought 'em off for a bit."

Williams grinned. "Thanks, Sergeant. It never occurred to me to run. You kept firing so fast I didn't think of anything but working the gun. I kind of enjoyed it."

108

It was almost dark when a squad of Captain Jones' artillerymen came over to relieve us. I hurried down to where Captain Pettit was detailing the men to set up tents for Company B. Sergeant Calvin had drawn rations for my squad and they were cooking supper, a meal that had to take the place of the noon meal we'd missed while working our six-pounder. I was hoping to find Frank Pierce. He was almost too tired to smile when I welcomed him back.

"When last I saw you, you'd almost caught up with the tail end of the Indian ponies. You should have caught one so you could ride. And the last time I heard you, you were all of a mile ahead of us yelling, 'Come on, come on!' "

He grinned but his voice was a whisper, "We had to stop and come back just when we had 'em routed. There were lodgepoles, robes, and dried meat scattered for ten miles. Their warriors were overrunning the women and their gear. But we were almost out of bullets — and all out of water. I almost lost two of my men from the heat. Dandin and Wiley got sick with chills after the excitement was over. But we had a good run. I think we shook 'em a bit, today."

"And it sounds like you yelled yourself hoarse."

He grinned happily. That ended our day of regrouping on the next day after the Battle of Big Mound. We put out extra pickets and extra guards for the horses. About midnight it began to rain. In the morning it cleared for a spell. Then the eastern sky turned black and it began to pour, just as scouts reported the approach of a still bigger mass of savages.

Captain Pettit was worried. "This could be serious if the savages ever learn that our artillery is useless in a rainstorm," he warned us. "Keep covers on your muskets."

Colonel McPhail led the forward defense with the help of cavalry and two of Captain Jones' howitzers. Just as

109

the Colonel raised his saber for a charge up the ridge, another shaft of lightning crackled across the sky. It seemed to sparkle off the tip of his sword like a bursting grenade. As he fell from his horse, the scene was cut off from us by a sheet of rain. Even the hill was out of sight. I'd already covered our six-pounder to keep it as dry as possible. Above the almost continuous firing of guns rolled the volleys of thunder. Lightning crackled louder than Jones' fieldpiece. I couldn't understand how he could continue firing. I knew that I'd have to draw the charge and reload our gun before we could fire. Later we learned that by some freak of the storm, his two guns were in only a light rain, while our troops and the Indians were soaked by heavy showers.

Then the worst of the storm was blown to the west. The sun came out and General Sibley trotted through camp on his big black jumper, breaking up the encampment and urging us forward. Occasionally, Indians would appear on the ridges ahead and prepare to charge. We'd swing our six-pounders into position and they'd flitter away behind the ridge. By fits and starts we marched for several miles. About the middle of the afternoon there was a new threat of battle in front of us. Jones wheeled his fieldpieces into position and threw spherical case shot at extreme range at the massed Indians. A few were unhorsed. A squadron of our cavalry drove in on their flank and they fled.

It was about that time that Colonel Crooks came up with the reason for their several feints and futile attacks. They were trying to draw us away from a clump of brush and trees at the foot of some cliffs. The families of many of the warriors had been overtaken and were hiding in the brush with their camp gear. General Sibley ordered Colonal Crooks to take two companies of infantry and burn the woods to destroy their gear. The women and old men were already climbing up the cliffs toward a rugged mountain of boulders to get away. We could have shot them but not one shot was fired.

Their supplies were found in scattered heaps where the Indians had dropped them. Presently, Colonel Crooks' men got the pitchpine woods afire, even though it had been raining. Pine trees and dead grass make a hot fire. Lodgepoles, blankets, and fat pemmican burned — along with lice, fleas, and bedbugs.

Captain Jones was standing near me, where we'd placed a six-pounder for support. While we watched the destruction, we listened to the crackling flames.

"Hear those bedbugs pop when they burn, Captain? They're so full of oil from fat squaws they're like popcorn."

"It may be only the pitch popping, but that's the way to break up this Indian uprising. Now those squaws will want to head back to the reservation after treaty beef and money. Later, they'll be just as quick to urge another raid."

"Will a good licking send the warriors back?"

"Nothing else will. They still think we're too busy with the Great Rebellion to bother with defending the western settlements. They'd rather raid farms than to grow food or hunt for it. They're dirty, lazy, and completely without morals. They raid each other just as they raid settlers. They have never used any of the prairie for peaceable living and they never will. They're of no use to the country and not much to themselves.

"Until they are forced to produce something to eat and learn that working can give more certainty of food than stealing it, they'll be like they are now — rats in our granary."

"You've been fighting the rats a long time, Captain. Do any ever learn to farm instead of steal and fight?"

"The Mexicans down below Texas were a lot like the Sioux, but they've turned to farming. We had to whip 'em in Texas in 1836 and then we had the big fight in 1846 but they learned. Now they're moving into Texas by the hundreds to work on the cattle ranches. Mostly, they're pretty good help."

111

I felt that the Sioux would turn out to be harder to civilize than the Mexicans, but I had to agree with what he'd said.

On that 26th of July we marched and fought for more than twelve miles, finally camping at Stony Lake. It must have been evident to General Sibley and his staff that our horses were too worn out to pursue Indians any further until we'd rested.

Besides needing rest, we had to find out where they were. After the Battle of Big Mound the one large band had been pushed west. The fight near Dead Buffalo Lake had driven a camp of several thousand lodges over the mountain and to the south. (That term "lodge" also included families without any covering, for we'd burned hundreds of lodges and buffalo robes with their poles, camp gear, and sacks of dried meat.) We'd raised hob with their winter supplies but most of the Indians had gotten away by climbing up over the boulders and through ravines far too rough for guns, or even cavalry to follow.

All we were sure of was that they were south of Stony Lake where we encamped for the night. But we didn't have long to rest. Scouts told us that the Sioux women were howling in despair over the loss of their dried meat, bags of tallow, and buffalo robes. They were caterwauling over the loss of lodges and cooking utensils. In the next few days the loss of other precious belongings had them caterwauling and shrieking at the warriors who had failed them.

We felt pretty good. We'd made a big strike. Then somehow the separated bands of Sioux were able to circle ahead of us and join forces. Perhaps the General should have pushed his advantage when he had the bands separated. For his defense, it must be said that some of his infantry had marched and fought Indians for more than eighty miles in four days. In addition, some of those men had been doing picket duty, breaking camp, and making camp, working for sixteen to twenty hours a day.

112

Most of those hours had been hot and tiring, with uncertainty dogging our heels. We'd been short of water, and the water in both Dead Buffalo Lake and Stony Lake had been tepid and tasting of marshgrass and mud. Mounted infantry might have kept the Indian bands separated and on the run. Our cavalry were more than a match for the Indians in the open prairie, but this was broken country where the Indian was at his best.

It was important strategy to push the Indians. It was even more important to prevent a major defeat for the white man. If they could have broken our lines, even once, or silenced our artillery, we'd have been overwhelmed by numbers within a few minutes. The knowledge of that fact made us fight like demons; it also put a constant fear into the heart of the bravest soldier.

We were nearing the end of the campaign. That afternoon General Sibley made us a speech, standing on the caisson beside Captain Jones' fieldpiece. It was an inspiring effort. He ended with, "Now that you have seen that it is possible to whip the Sioux, even when we are outnumbered; now that you have seen their cowardly tactics of murdering, even while they are pretending friendship, let nothing stop us from destroying their security and pushing them across the Missouri. Deny them every resource — even one gun, a horse, or a blanket. We must double our pickets, defeat their every ambush, fight to the death to protect our wagons. None of them shall get close enough to have the advantage of their hatchets and spears.

"You have been a superb troop. Not one man has fled in time of danger. If there is a difference among you it is only in the degree of skill and bravery as soldiers that you have shown. Some of you have gone beyond the calling of heroes. Captain Jones has repeatedly broken the massed charge of the savages, when it was only the steady rain of his canister that was able to stop their rushing attacks. Our cavalry have been in the forefront of attack, just as our artillerymen have never flinched from the hottest fire.

113

It can never be said that our infantrymen have ever failed to support with the highest bravery the efforts of others.

"Now we are close to the final days of our attack. The Missouri River is only a long day's march away. There we are to meet with General Sully for the final defeat of the Sioux. Let us drive forward with our best speed. Let us put such confusion into the retreat of the Sioux that we will sweep them like rats into the trap that General Sully has prepared."

And there was a mighty cheer as the General stepped down from the caisson. Colonels McPhail and Crooks stepped forward to shake his hand, but McPhail had to use his left hand. His right was bandaged to cover the burn from the stroke of lightning when his saber had been burnt up. He was lucky to be alive. An infantryman had been killed by the same stroke.

Captain Jones came over to where Williams and I were supervising the cleaning of our six-pounder. "Be ready at daylight to break camp," he said. We are to support the Tenth Regiment with two six-pounders in the main advance. I will take charge of the guns on the left. Lieutenant Whipple will support the right with howitzers. We'll sweep everything before us. The most dangerous half-hour will be when the separate companies move out to take up their line of march."

I cannot explain the uncanny judgment of Captain Jones. Of course he had seen many attacks by Indians. And he had immense faith in the damage his guns could do and in the riflemen supporting him. He had seemed to be without fear in the face of the heaviest musket fire. Some said he had a charmed life. But he had a tremendous defense in the fire-power of his guns. He depended on breaking the enemy before they could get close enough for accurate shooting. His theories were proven by the fewness of our men who were wounded — and no artillerymen were killed. More of our men died of illness and accidents than were killed by the bullets and arrows of the Sioux, on the whole campaign.

114

But the campaign did not end with General Sibley's speech. As we were breaking camp next morning, hordes of Indians appeared on the hills around us. Waves of them tried to charge our camp before we could form defensive lines. My two guns were emplaced on a low mound, around which the two companies of the Tenth were forming. For a hot half-hour we rained spherical-case shells, and then canister into the charging mass of savages, while more of the Tenth poured into trenches near us for our support.

I could hear the regular boom of both Jones' and Whipple's guns, and the crackle and snarl as our shells burst among the Indians. By the time we had softened the fury of the charge in front of us, there was a solid mass of savages in a great circle around us. In our rear, the Seventh Regiment, with the support of men who hadn't time to join their own companies, were holding off waves of Indians and getting the wagons under way inside our supporting lines of men.

Suddenly we had no more masses of Indians within range of our six-pounders. Sergeant Williams wiped the sweat from his forehead and asked, "Why don't we form a circle for defense? We have water. We can't keep moving and fight 'em off."

"I expect the General is after their lodges and supplies. If we stop, they'll slip across the Missouri and get away. In that broken country we'd never catch them. And we'd lose a lot of men crossing the Missouri under their fire. We have to keep pushing hard enough to overrun their families, burn their lodges, and kill enough of them to make them sorry they murdered white people. Our best defense will be to keep the devils off balance and retreating. Then we'll push the whole nation of Sioux into the river."

And that's what we tried to do. The impossible task is easy to look back on. We continually forced the warriors to overrun their squaws and old men. That put them on the defensive and made them frantic. Under our desperate

115

counterattacks on their center, we pressed the warriors into ineffective mobs. We were close to disaster a dozen times but the speed of our attack defeated them. Not all of us had the strength of Frank Pierce, or the pressing indestructibility of Captain Jones. Somehow, Sergeant Williams was able to keep track of our ammunition and where to get more. With his carefulness we had case shells and powder for every flurry of fighting. Twice I saw some of the Fourth Platoon men staggering up with loads of cartridges for Frank Pierce. He fought like a madman, as did his men.

By noon our lines were strung out for more than a mile. A fieldpiece on my left was silent for many minutes as it crossed a ravine and had to be dragged up a ridge to a new emplacement. Even that one silent gun let the ring of Indians around us increase their fire to a fury. A six-pounder broke a wheel in crossing a gully. Another wheel had to be brought up from a supply wagon. Then a howitzer became a tangle of gun and mules when the men were unable to slow it enough in a descent into a steep-sided ravine. One mule had to be shot. Men had to take its place to frantically drag the gun up the next ridge and into position.

By mid-afternoon I could no longer think, but we pressed on. From the top of a ridge ahead of us a man suddenly cheered and waved his cap. Then the whole company near him broke into cheers. We hurried up onto the ridge. Far away, we could see the sun glinting on a wide river, winding in meandering curves among a maze of woods and mudbanks. But even while we cheered, we knew that it was still miles — and many hours away. But after that encouraging sight there was no way to slow us down. Company after company took up the cheering as soon as they came in sight of the mighty Missouri.

Our shouting seemed to sap the strength of the Indians. They still circled and charged stubbornly, as one or another of our advancing lines cut off the retreat of their

116

gear-laden families. Some of them were reluctant to leave the thickets into which they had been driven. They'd try to hide their belongings before racing on to another clump of trees. While our leading companies fought off their attacks, the infantry guarding the wagons took the time to burn the thickets and the hidden gear.

Our orders were to leave all of the Sioux east of the Missouri destitute. It was the only way to make them regret the murder of the whites. And it was one way to separate the warlike ones from those who had remained on the reservation.

The clumps of brush and trees were becoming more numerous as we swept down the ridges toward the river. Couriers from General Sibley warned us to hold back our leaders and to shape up the line of march. We were glad to close ranks and to fight more warily. Driving the savages into the river was exciting but we were exhausted. We often saw horses lying in the gullies, too worn out to climb the bank of the ravine.

Then, as a little breeze from the river began to break the hellish heat of that exhausting afternoon, a new order came to shift to the southeast. Presently we were ordered to encamp on the Apple River. Most of the infantrymen were allowed to rest. The Rangers and cavalry of the Seventh Regiment were sent out on picket duty, and to scout the activity of the Sioux.

We in the artillery had marched and fought an incredible twenty-five miles — with no food since a light breakfast and no water excepting the little in our canteens.

Naturally, many of us were too tired to eat. We lay like the dead, until hardier brothers brought us food and cool water. Some, Frank Pierce among them, who had fought like demons, still had the strength to nurse those who had sickened in the heat. He had carried exhausted men to the wagons to be cared for by the teamsters. He seemed to be in the middle of every fight. I have wondered at his endurance. When I tried to praise him, he would only shrug.

117

"You were half-dead when you got back to camp at Big Mound, Frank. Tonight, you're still going strong. The men all agree that we marched and fought over twenty-four miles today. You went farther than that — back and forth. How?"

"It's all in your head, boy," he grinned. "I like to keep pressing on, like we did today."

"Well, we've sure pushed 'em. How did they get away?"

"They know this country. We were climbing up and down; they were taking the paths we didn't see. But it was a great drive. I enjoyed every minute. We were going downhill more than up. My boys take downhill going better."

"How did Wiley and Dandin get along on the march?"

"Pretty fair. They've learned real fast not to run in the heat of the day. They'll do real well chasing Indians. It was the dryness made 'em sick before."

And we'd all learned to take it easier. That was our last day of all-out fighting. We'd set out to crush the Sioux. Now we were willing to relax.

Colonel Crooks' patrol came back and reported large bands of Indians in the woods on our side, and that the hills across the river were black with people. But there were only a few lodges.

On the next day, Wednesday, the 29th, Colonel Mc-Phail's cavalry and two six-pounders under Captain Jones went upriver to clear the woods on our side. Without losing a man, in spite of harassment by musketeers, they destroyed wagons, lodges, and tons of dried meat. Getting close to the river, they saw women, children, and warriors struggling across the turbulent stream. They were using canoes, logs, and any supporting brush they could find. Warriors were swimming across, hanging to horses' tails.

As Frank commented, — "Riding a horse across the Missouri is a trick I'd hate to attempt. It's too muddy to see whether the edge of the mud bank is a foot deep or over your head. And the sand keeps pulling you deeper

118

in the water. I'd want a strong horse. The Indian ponies are mostly small and starved."

(Reports of Brig. General Henry H. Sibley, Commanding)[13]

EXPEDITION AGAINST THE SIOUX INDIANS, HEADQUARTERS DISTRICT OF MINNESOTA, Camp Carter, Bank of the James River, Aug. 7, 1863. MAJOR (Adjutant to Major General John Pope): My last dispatch was dated 21st ultimo, from Camp Olin, in which I had the honor to inform (you) that I had left one-third of my force in an intrenched position at Camp Atchison, and was then one day's march in advance, with 1,400 infantry and 500 cavalry, in the direction where the main body of the Indians was supposed to be.

During the three days following I pursued a course somewhat west of south, making 50 miles, having crossed the James river and the Great Coteau of the Missouri. On the 25th, about 1 P.M., being considerably in advance of the main column, with some of the officers of my staff, engaged in looking for a suitable camping ground, the command having marched steadily since 5 A.M., some of my scouts came to me at full speed, and reported that a large camp of Indians had just been passed and great numbers of warriors could be seen upon the prairie, two or three miles distant. I immediately corralled my train upon the shore of a salt lake nearby, and established my camp, which was rapidly intrenched by Colonel Crooks, to whom was entrusted that duty, for the security of the transportation in case of attack, a precaution I had taken whenever we encamped for many days previously. While the earthworks were being pushed forward, parties of Indians, more or less numerous, appeared upon the hills around us, and one of my half-breed scouts, a relative of Red Plume, a Sisseton chief, hitherto opposed to the war, approached sufficiently near to converse with him. Red

119

Plume told him to warn me that the plan was to invite me to a council, with some of my superior officers, to shoot us without ceremony, and then attack my command in great force, trusting to destroy the whole of it. The Indians ventured near the spot where a portion of my scouts had taken position, 300 or 400 yards from our camp, and conversed with them in apparently friendly fashion, some of them professing a desire for peace. Surg(eon) Josiah S. Weiser, of the First Regiment Minnesota Mounted Rangers, incautiously joined the group of scouts, when a young savage, doubtless supposing from his uniform and horse equipments that he was an officer of rank, pretended great friendship and delight at seeing him, but within a few feet treacherously shot him through the heart. The scouts discharged their pieces at the murderer, but he escaped, leaving his horse behind. The body of Dr. Weiser was immediately brought to camp, unmutilated, save by the ball that killed him. He was universally esteemed, being skillful in his profession and a courteous gentleman.

This outrage precipitated an immediate engagement. The savages in great numbers, concealed by the ridges, had encircled that portion of the camp not flanked by the lake referred to, and commenced an attack. Colonel (Samuel) McPhail, with two companies, subsequently re-enforced by others, as they could be spared from other points, was directed to drive the enemy from the hill where Dr. Weiser was shot. . . . Taking with me a 6-pounder, under the command of Lieut. (John J.) Whipple, I ascended a hill toward Big Mound, on the opposite side of the ravine, and opened fire with spherical-case shot upon the Indians, who had obtained possession of the upper part of the large ravine, and of the smaller ones tributary to it, under the protection of which they could annoy the infantry and cavalry without exposure on their part. This flank and raking fire of artillery drove them from their hiding places into the broken prairie. . . .

The savages were steadily driven from one strong position after another, under severe fire, until, feeling their utter inability to contend longer with our soldiers in the open field, they joined their brethren in one common flight. Upon moving forward with my staff to a commanding point which overlooked the field, I discovered the whole body of Indians, numbering from 1,000 to 1,500, retiring in confusion from the combat, while a dark line of moving objects on the distant hills indicated the location of their families. I immediately dispatched orders to Colonel McPhail, who had now received an accession of force from the other companies of his mounted regiment, to press on with all expedition and fall upon the rear of the enemy, but not to pursue after nightfall. . . . The order to Colonel McPhail was improperly delivered, as requiring him to return to camp, instead of bivouacking on the prairie. Consequently he retraced his way with his weary men and horses, followed by the still more weary infantry, and arrived at camp early the next morning, as I was about to move forward with the main column. Thus ended the battle of "Big Mound." The severity of the labors . . . the engagement commenced after the day's march was nearly completed, and that the Indians were chased at least 12 miles, making altogether full 40 miles performed without rest, was most exhausting.

The march of the cavalry of the Seventh Regiment and Company B of the Tenth Regiment, in returning to camp after the tremendous efforts of the day, is almost unparalleled. . . . Upon arriving at the camp from which the Indians had been driven in such hot haste, vast quantities of dried meat, tallow, and buffalo robes, cooking utensils, and other indispensable articles were found concealed in the long reeds around the lake, all of which were by my direction collected and burned. For miles along the route the prairie was strewn with like evidence of hasty flight. Colonel McPhail had previously informed me that beyond Dead Buffalo Lake, as far

121

as his pursuit of the Indians had continued, I would find neither wood nor water. I consequently established my camp on the border of that lake, and very soon afterward parties of Indians made their appearance, threatening an attack. I directed Captain (John) Jones to repair with his section of 6-pounders, supported by Captain (Jonathan) Chase, with his company of pioneers, to a commanding point about 600 yards in advance, and I proceeded in person to the same point. I there found Colonel McPhail, who had taken position with two companies of his regiment, commanded by Captain Grant and Lieutenant Grant, to check the advance of the Indians in that quarter. An engagement ensued, at long range, the Indians being too wary to attempt to close, although greatly superior in numbers. The spherical-case shot from the 6-pounders soon caused a hasty retreat from that locality, but perceiving it to be their intention to make a flank movement on the left of the camp in force (I) swung my forces to meet them . . . but the increasing numbers of the Indians, who were well mounted, enabled them by a circuitous route to dash toward the extreme left of the camp, evidently with a view to stampede the mules herded on the shore of the lake. This daring attempt was frustrated by the rapid motions of the Mounted Rangers, commanded by Captains (Eugene M.) Wilson and (Peter B.) Davy, who met the enemy and repulsed them with loss . . . and the battle of "Dead Buffalo Lake" was ended.

On . . . the 28th, there took place the greatest conflict between our troops and the Indians, so far as numbers were concerned, which I have named the battle of "Stony Lake.". . . part of the wagons were still in camp, under the guard of the Seventh Regiment, when I perceived a large force of mounted Indians moving rapidly upon us. 1 immediately sent orders to the several commands to assume their posisions. . . . The Tenth gallantly checked the advance of the enemy in front; the Sixth and the cavalry on

122

the right, and the Seventh and the cavalry on the left, while the 6-pounders and two sections of mountain howitzers under the efficient direction of their respective chiefs, poured a rapid and destructive fire from as many different points. The vast number of Indians enabled them to form two-thirds of a circle, five or six miles in extent, along the whole of which they were seeking for some weak point upon which to precipitate themselves. The firing was rapid and incessant from each side; but as soon as I had completed the details of the designated order of march, and closed up the train, the column issued in line of battle upon the prairie, in the face of the immense force opposed to it, and I resumed my march without any delay. This proof of confidence in our own strength completely destroyed the hopes of the savages.

This engagement was the last desperate effort of the combined Dakota bands to prevent the further advance on our part toward their families. It would have been difficult to estimate the number of warriors, but no cool and dispassionate observer would probably have placed it at less than 2,200 to 2,500. . . . the remnants of the bands who escaped with Little Crow had successively joined the Sissetons, the Cut-heads, and finally the Yanktonais, the most powerful single band of the Dakotas, and together with all these, had formed an enormous camp of nearly, or quite, 10,000 souls. . . .

When we went into camp on the banks of the Apple river a few mounted Indians could alone be seen. Early in the morning I dispatched Colonel McPhail with the companies of the Mounted Rangers and the two 6-pounders, to harass and retard the retreat of the Indians across the Missouri River, and followed with the main column as rapidly as possible. We reached the woods on the border of that stream shortly after noon on the 29th, but the Indians had crossed their families during the preceeding night, and it took but a short time for the men to follow them on their ponies.

The hills on the opposite side were covered by the men, and they had probably formed the determination to oppose our passage of the river, both sides of which were here covered with a dense growth of underbrush and timber for more than a mile. I dispatched Colonel Crooks with his regiment, which was in advance, to clear the woods to the river of Indians. . . .

There being no water on the prairie, I proceeded down the Missouri to the nearest point on the Apple river, opposite Burnt Boat Island, and made my camp. The following day Colonel Crooks, with a strong detachment of eleven companies of infantry and dismounted cavalry and three guns, under the command of Captain Jones, was dispatched to destroy the property left in the woods, which was thoroughly performed. . . . From 120 to 150 wagons and carts were thus disposed of. . . . I waited two days in camp, hoping to open communications with General Sully, who, with his comparatively fresh mounted force, could easily have followed up and destroyed the enemy we had so persistently hunted. The long and rapid marches which had so debilitated the infantry, and the horses and mules employed in the transportation, had led to utter exhaustion. Under the circumstances, I felt that this column had done everything possible. . . . For three successive evenings I caused the cannon to be fired and signal rockets sent up, but all these elicited no reply from General Sully, and I am apprehensive he has been detained by insurmountable obstacles. The point struck by me on the Missouri is about 40 miles below Fort Clarke, in latitude 46°42′, longitude 100°35′.

The military results of the expedition have been highly satisfactory. A march of nearly 600 miles from St. Paul has been made, in a season of fierce heats and unprecedented draught, when even the most experienced voyagers predicted the impossibility of such a movement. A vigilant and powerful, as well as confident, enemy was found, successively routed in three different engagements, with a loss of at least

124

150 killed and wounded of his best and bravest warriors, and his beaten forces driven in confusion and dismay, with the sacrifice of vast quantities of subsistence, clothing, and means of transportation, across the Missouri river. . . .

The March Home

We all felt pretty good about that campaign. It was only much later that we realized that we should have crushed the Sioux as they tried to cross the Missouri. We'd killed hundreds, we should have pressed them harder as they crossed the Missouri and killed thousands. Actually, the Indian women were as much to be blamed as the warriors. The squaws we'd seen back in Minnesota were usually wearing soiled and torn dresses that had once belonged to some white woman who had taken pride in her clean linen and pretty clothing. We treated the Indians like animals because they lived like animals and raided our settlements like the wolves and coyotes we used for comparison.

While we were camped on the Apple River we heard some news that put life into our march back to Minnesota. The Union victories at Vicksburg and Gettysburg on July 4th were announced by a squad of scouts from General Sully's brigade as soon as they rode into our camp. The scouts had been coming west in considerable fear of the

Sioux ahead of them, when they heard the cannonading of Captain Jones' battery as he drove the Indians out of the dense thickets of prickly ash and blackberry briars on the northeast bank of the Missouri.

Moving cautiously toward the noise, they had come onto our encampment. They reported that General Sully had been floating supplies up the river in small boats because low water had stopped the river steamers. Hence his delay in meeting us. He was reluctant to move ahead of his supplies. It might be a week before he would get to this point.

There were a great many rumors, suggestions, and free advice bandied around our camp while we rested. General Sibley settled the matter in his own way on the third morning. Since we had barely enough supplies to last us until we got to Minnesota, we'd start at once. We didn't have the men and ammunition to complete a long trek into the hills after the fleeing Sioux. Our only sensible plan was to hurry back to Camp Atchison, pick up the supplies not needed for that post, and go on home. Then we could send supplies north to Fort Abercrombie and other posts.

The Sixth Regiment Minnesota Volunteers was urgently needed to fill Minnesota's quota of trained men to fight in the Mississippi campaign. When General Sibley made his speech we cheered him wildly — he was telling us to do what we wanted most — go home.

At Camp Atchison we learned that the wagon train intended for the mining camp of Bannack on Grasshopper Creek had been diverted to a new strike in Alder Gulch, called Virginia City. There had been a big rush of miners from other camps and they badly needed the supplies. Several rich strikes had been made in July and August, 1863, while we'd been chasing the Sioux across Dakota Territory and the Missouri River.

People back home have wondered why the army, that was straining every muscle to whip the rebels, still had men and supplies for a brigade to chase Indians, and ride herd on wagon trains going to the goldfields. The answer is that the Union needed gold. Millions of dollars worth

127

of nuggets were being shipped back east from California, Idaho, Colorado, and Montana. That gold bolstered our currency and let us buy needed supplies from England — which traded with the Confederate States also and thought it brave to run our naval blockade.

Every ounce of gold was important to the progress of the war. Every farmer on the frontier was needed to raise more food for the men in uniform. The uprising of the Sioux had been a severe blow to our economy. All the cattle and horses stolen by the Sioux were that much loss to the Union. We had done our best to prevent such an uprising again.

Thus ended the Campaign against the Sioux in 1863.

The Sioux Campaign Of 1864

Sauk Centre, Tuesday, May 17th, 1864[14]

Dear Wife: It has been a week since you left here and
nothing has happened. . . . Three Companies arrived
from Fort Ripley and today one more, Co. H, with
our ponies. I have just been down to see them and
they look like so many sheep, but they have been
poorly cared for. There is plenty of them that don't
weight five hunderd pounds. . . .

From your affectionate husband. F. Pierce.

But with the coming of spring in 1864, the powers that
be discovered that we had not punished the Indians
enough. Small bands of the Sissiton Sioux from the villages
under White Lodge and other militant chiefs continued to
raid the settlements for horses, cattle, and hostages. Anything left by the absent settlers was stolen or destroyed.
Small wagon trains were often attacked and the drivers

killed and the goods stolen. Company B was sent to Sauk Centre to parade in the streets, and we made several trips with wagon trains to Alexandria and Fort Abercrombie.

In February, Frank Pierce was taken sick with lung fever and nearly died. His colds had gotten worse and he'd taken pneumonia. In late April, his wife, Caroline, had come up to Sauk Centre to see him. He was overjoyed to see her but she did not enjoy taking care of a sick person. In a few weeks she went back to Freeborn and Frank came back to our barracks. He was as thin as a rail but managed to take over his duties.

There had been a good many down with colds, pneumonia, and dysentery. I'd been drawing rations for both our platoons. Two of his corporals, Buck and Ginattoney, had been sick for several weeks. We'd hoped that this would be the last winter that we'd have to sleep in tents, but as it turned out we lived in tents all of the time I was in the army. There was always a new post to be built, or our company would be sent out on an Indian campaign or to retrieve horses. There were always wagon trains to guard, and we'd had experience in those things. The new volunteers would be sent to take over the posts we'd built.

There was one change that pleased all of us in Company B. The generals in charge of the Indian campaign had finally decided that we couldn't walk fast enough to catch Indians on ponies. So they got us some ponies about the middle of May, and we became what they called mounted infantry. Now we could chase Indians on horseback and use the ponies for carrying much of our supplies on the march.

We weren't asked to learn much about cavalry tactics. In the first place, it takes longer to train a cavalry horse than a cavalryman. If there was to be any fighting out in the open, the companies of regular cavalry with the brigade could charge and countercharge to their hearts' content. But most of the fighting in 1863 had boiled down to defending the wagons, or to chasing Indians over the country

130

that was too rough or wooded for maneuvers. Usually, the cavalry fought dismounted.

On the 28th of May, 1864, we were assigned to the Eighth Regiment Minnesota Volunteers and sent to Fort Ridgley. Captain Jones was there, and again I was assigned to duty with his battery (Third Minnesota) to train gun crews. He still had only eight field-guns and howitzers, but there were all new crews to learn to use them. And we had only about ten days in which to get them skilled in loading, bracing, and aiming the guns.

On June 6th, we left Fort Ridgley under Colonel Thomas to go to Swan Lake to meet General Sully, who had charge of the whole campaign against the Sioux. This time we were to drive them out of the hills along the Missouri and chase them west of the Rockies. Frank Pierce beamed when he saw me helping to get a six-pounder ready to roll. He was riding a little sorrel gelding with a blazed face. It was stepping right along under his 160 pounds and almost as much weight in gear. His Sharps rifle was just as clean as on the day he'd brought it to Fort Ridgley two years before. But it was shiny from wear and cleaning.

"You ought to be carrying that pony, Frank," and I smiled at his wide grin. "You're bigger than it is."

"You just watch this horse. He's got more life than the Captain's big chestnut ever had. On this trip I won't have to eat dust from your mules."

"For that rabbit-sized horse, it's a good thing you've lost some weight since we joined this army."

"I've gained back more than twenty pounds since I was able to get up and around. As soon as we get some of those good and tough buffalo steaks I'll pick up faster. It sure is nice to eat my way back up to my old weight."

I was glad for him. There had been a few weeks in March when I didn't think he'd ever campaign again. He was still thin but almost as full of energy as ever. He'd been drilling new men steadily for three weeks. If he could stand that, this campaign should invigorate him all the more. He liked marching.

131

On the first day of our march west, we had the usual mixture of heat and dust. Men got lost and companies mixed up. Colonel Thomas had been on two campaigns and he got things organized quicker than General Sibley ever did. But he wasn't as patient. Some of the language he used on the new officers must have burned their ears. Certainly, Captain Jones kept a watchful eye on all of the new men in the battery, to make sure they were in line and wide awake.

That night our battery set up camp with the Second Minnesota Cavalry, under Colonel MacLaren, near the front of the column, and led the line of march for three days.

On the 9th of June we overtook an emigrant train of 160 wagons bound for the goldfields in Montana. There were men, women, and children in the party. That slowed us down some, but on the 21st we crossed the James River, and on July 1st we arrived at Camp 18 on the Missouri, in a downpour of rain. General Sully's brigade had arrived there only the day before, using riverboats. We crossed to the west side of the Missouri in their boats. In the rain and mud it was hard to tell where the river left off and the sloppy banks began. To their surprise, some of the men in Captain Jones' squad stepped off onto what looked like the shore of mud and landed up to their waists in the river. While we were unloading the fieldpieces, the mire grew deeper and tempers short. It was a warm rain but we were glad to get tents put up and fires going to help us dry out.

Frank's platoon set up camp with mine. All our horses were corralled with the horses and mules of the battery. My assignment to help Captain Jones drill his recruits into old campaigners was in addition to looking after my own squad. It wasn't easy. Capt. Jones had been given a dozen paroled rebels who had offered to fight in the Indian campaign. We'd had to watch like hawks to prevent their escape to work their way south. Most of them were sullen and slack. He got his camp set up with almost no help

132

from them. They were supposed to help work the guns, but all they were good for was to help the horseboys graze and corral the mules. A corporal with a loaded rifle had to oversee that.

Toward sunset, after the rain had stopped, he came over to the gun park where the Johnnies were wiping down the mule harnesses, and spoke to Sergeant Williams, in charge of the work.

"Don't waste any more time keeping these rebels from trying to desert, Sergeant. It's a long thousand miles to where they have any friends. If they'll help fight Indians, fine. If they run away, we won't have to feed them."

Then he turned to the rebel who seemed to be a leader of the bunch, "Start doing your share and we'll get along fine. Desert, and your scalps'll be hanging at the belt of a Sioux warrior before night. They're all around those hills to the south and east. And they don't take men prisoners."

That ended their trying to get away. They never worked very hard until we'd had our first battle with the Sioux. In that conflict they looked just as scared as I felt — and they fought just as hard. Once, when we were almost overrun by a mass of the devils, I saw one Johnnie club three warriors to break his way back to our group — with tears of fear and anger streaming down his face. Being scared was not the mark of a coward in that fight.

One of them, called Russ Turner, even became friendly enough to ask if I was from near Louisville, Tennessee.

"I knew a Hartley Morgan from there."

"That might have been my brother, Hartley," I said.

"He was in Jackson's Brigade. How come you're fighting for the Union?" — he wanted to know.

"Because I prefer the Union. How did you get in here?"

"After most of our company was captured at Fredricksburg, we were sent to a camp above New York. We gave parole so we could get west. We planned to head for Texas. Now I'm glad we didn't try it. I've been talking

133

with a fellow who saw what happened back in Iowa, in a massacre. Believe me, I want an army with me when I see any Indians. Those settlers never had a chance. Was it like that in Minnesota?"

"Worse. The Indians would beg for food, eat it, and when the white family was off guard they'd murder them — or worse."

"Did you actually know of any murder and assault?"

"Certainly. Most of our men in Company B were there at that time. We were in two battles at Fort Ridgley. We could have gone home after that. But we chose to stay and fight Indians. And we've killed quite a few, but nowhere near the five hundred settlers who were murdered. We may have a chance to even up the score a little on this campaign.

"But this won't end the damage. Indians will still ambush emigrant trains and murder homesteaders and miners whenever they can. We'll whip 'em this summer — and then have it to do all over again next year. Yes sir, I can match any story you ever heard and give names and places. They are still learning more about how the Indians tortured women and mutilated babies. Wait till you see the fresh scalps of little girls when we capture any Indian guns and lances! I'll kill every Sioux I can."

On the second day after that, General Sully headed west with most of his two brigades. Word had come that 1,800 lodges of Sioux were camped on the Cannon Ball River. Most of the army wagons and supplies were left there at Fort Rice, as General Sully named this new post. He laid out plans for fortifications and set some of the men to building a warehouse and barricades. From the entrenchments he laid out, he must have planned on its being the major post in the area, both to subdue the Indians and to supply emigrant trains going west. It was to have a landing for riverboats and log buildings.

I was glad to be on the move again, but I was sorry that we had to leave Frank Pierce at Fort Rice. Lung

134

fever had left him too weak to ride his horse. Fortunately, his platoon, with new rifles, including some Sharps, were attached to mine to support Jones' battery. The Sioux had plenty of reason to fear and hate our six-pounders. We were certain to be the goal for most of their massed charges. But Frank's training paid off. His men gave us good protection — and the massed Indians gave us the targets for our artillery.

The next month was one I'd like to forget. We left Fort Rice on the 20th of July and marched west along the Heart River with a force of nearly 2,200 men. That had been the route for wagon trains heading for the Idaho goldfields. Game was scarce and every night there was less grass for our stock. We missed Frank, and the game he could always find.

More than a score of men from the infantry had been sick with fevers and sore eyes. They were still able to help at the fort and protect it from stray Indians and wolves. With game scarce, the wolves were hunting in packs of over a hundred. They'd come right into camp and try to pull down a horse. The wolves usually left the quick-kicking mules alone.

There was one consolation in Frank's staying at Fort Rice. I'm sure he'd have died on our march with General Sully, who had never gotten over the bad report he'd had for failing to meet General Sibley at the Missouri in 1863. We'd heard rumors that Colonel Thomas had defended General Sibley's action, and it was apparent that General Sully never spoke to him except to give orders and censure.

Our Minnesota brigade was always in hot water. We got the dirtiest work and the poorest food. We seemed to be permanently assigned to rear guard duty and the extra work with the supply wagons and emigrant train. The alkali dust and bad water had half of our men sick with sore eyes and heavy colds, but we couldn't stop or go back. We had to tough it out.

About the third day along Heart River, we got word

135

that 1,600 lodges of various Teton bands of the Sioux had moved from the Cannon Ball to the Knife River. That was rough country, with high hills and no roads for the heavy freight wagons.

General Sully ordered the wagons corralled. Supplies for the march to the Knife River were to be loaded on pack mules. But there were no saddle blankets in the supplies General Sully had brought along. The pack saddles fit poorly, and the gunny sacks General Sully ordered to be used were little better than nothing. Instead of webbing for cinchas, the commissary had sent sole leather belts. They were tried, but the mules promptly tore through camp, knocking down tents while kicking off their packs.

That foulup in the supplies couldn't be blamed on the Minnesota brigade, as I heard Colonel Thomas point out to General Sully. The General came close to apoplexy while the mules bucked and kicked the camp to pieces. He gave his staff a bad half-day and finally ordered us to take as few supplies as possible and load them in the lightest wagons. We finally left the corralled wagons about 3 P.M., on July 26th.

We spent the next two days helping the mules haul wagons up the steep hills, and in reloading wagons that had tipped over. The mules were getting meaner with every accident. The temper of the men was even worse. When we saw the Indian encampment about 10 A.M., on the second day, both men and mules were exhausted and very dry, but we were fighting mean. We'd been on the march since 4 A.M.

We'd made no effort to surprise the Indians. And they'd made no attempt to slip away. Their scouts had seen us and it was obvious that they were glad to catch us out in the open. We were bringing our rifles and supplies right up to their camp on the slope of Tahkahokuty Mountain. As we got closer it became evident to any soldier why they were so confident. There were thou-

136

sands of warriors facing us, either naked or in full-feathered regalia. The General's report that there were at least 5,000 or 6,000 warriors must have been a low estimate.

Massed groups covered the ridges in a line as long as our column and many times deeper. They were better mounted than we were, and that horde looked like all the savages in the west.

Our line of approach had been up through a rough valley that opened out into a wide saucer. They could charge downhill from three directions. As our forward line came out into the mouth of the valley, a chief shouted to his warriors massed on the ridge to our left. His charge was directed toward our officers in their fancy uniforms riding near Captain Pope's artillery. The cavalry leading the line of march scampered off to one side with the General's staff, and Pope's six-pounders and howitzers swung into position and blasted the savages with canister. Two companies of mounted infantry galloped forward to protect General Sully's staff and fired several volleys in good order. After that the firing was ragged but fast and furious.

As the Indians broke and then turned to run, our cavalry charged with beautifully regular lines to hit their flank. A good many Indians who had stopped to pick up their dead and wounded were cut down as they ran.

Then another mass of savages charged on our infantry. Our lines were wider now as we pressed forward out of the valley. Pope's artillery cut the savages to pieces. A third mass from ahead of our lines was hampered in their charge by those still retreating with their dead and wounded and by riderless horses. As the Indians retreated out of range of Pope's canister, he used spherical-case shells, at longer range. By noon our infantry was able to form by companies in the open saucer, giving support to the artillery. The rest of our cavalry were out in the open, helping to flank the retreating Indians and drive

137

them back to the slopes of the mountain. Once there, the Indians would break into small groups in the ravines, among the trees in areas too broken for cavalry maneuvers.

Captain Jones' artillery and our Eighth Minnesota Regiment had been detailed to guard the supply train and our rear. For once, we got a lucky break. We were able to fill our canteens from a clear stream coming down a joining ravine opposite the Indian encampment. But we weren't entirely happy. We could see part of the battle, but we'd had no way to expend our frustration of the past two days.

Then about the middle of the afternoon, just after Jones' battery was ordered forward and to the right to support Brackett's Minnesota Cavalry, massed Indians began to pour out of the timber behind us. This huge band, newcomers to the fight, were close to the supply wagons when Jones swung all but one gun into position to protect the wagons. (That one gun was able to turn the Indians charging Brackett, and support him until he could sweep them clear back to the base of the mountain.)

Our five guns under Sergeant Williams completely routed the newcomers with spherical-case shells. Part of the time, we had to fire over the heads of our own people. At the first lull in the charge, two of our six-pounders raced toward the center of the massed Indians and quickly swung into position to pour canister in a hail that mowed the tops of bushes for the whole width of the Indian line. Riflemen from Company B supported us nicely. Soon scores of Indians, in little besides warpaint and feathers, littered the ground.

Then Jones brought up two howitzers to where they could shell the ravines where the retreating savages were hiding. Presently we saw many of them climbing up the rocky sides of the ridges. Artillery targets were hard to find. Companies of the Eighth Minnesota that had been holding the left of the line swung around and helped cover our rear

138

while our wagons pulled forward for better protection. Our whole position had become much better. One company was detailed to clear the timber behind us. Another pushed forward to support our cavalry as it chased small bands up the ridges. Pope's artillery was still shelling Indians in the ravines. Many of the Indians were now busy pulling down their lodges. Only a few were able to carry away their camp gear as they fled.

By sundown the battle was a rout for the savages. We bivouacked on the battlefield. We'd been marching and fighting for more than sixteen hours with nothing to eat since breakfast. Luckily, none of us with Captain Jones' battery had guard duty.

But next morning we were routed out early. Captain Pettit's Company B, with Companies E and F, were detailed to destroy the enemy stores and camp gear. To quell any Indians still skulking in the area, Captain Jones put me in charge of a howitzer which I emplaced to shell the ravines above the Indian camp. While on that duty I had a chance to talk with Edward Patterson, fourth sergeant under Frank Pierce.

"Who were you looking for yesterday? I saw your platoon shifting forward several times, almost to where you could have been overrun by those savages."

"We were picking off the young leaders — like Sergeant Pierce always does. He says they're the ones who always stir up trouble. There'll be some fewer of them to make war talk this winter. It's the only way to stop the Sioux."

Frank's platoon was nearly all expert riflemen. Even though he hadn't been able to come on this part of the campaign, his teaching let his men carry out his plans to the letter.

We went at the business of destroying lodges, robes, and sacks of dried meat in the same grim way. War is a hard business. This had to be a war of extermination, if possible. When Corporal Higgens found a cracked spear with three blonde scalps nailed to it we lost any compunction about

139

routing the Sioux. Two of the scalps were short and curly, probably from the heads of mere children. Other scalps and the belongings of white people were found. We piled and burned all of them with the rest of the camp gear. Probably some wagon train that we didn't know about had been massacred.

While we were working ourselves to exhaustion to complete the destruction of the Indian camp, the rest of Sully's brigade pushed on to hunt down the routed Indians. We had more work than we could do in one day. The last sweep of Brackett's cavalry had chased the squaws and old men out of camp before they could save much of anything. Our biggest care was in piling the robes and gear so they would burn and still avoid getting lice and bedbugs all over us.

Captain Pettit kept making the rounds saying, "Handle those hides with a pole. If you feel any lice on you, get down to the creek and wash or we'll have lice in *our* camp. Use poles."

Finally he said, "We can't pile all of it. Set fire to the woods in a big circle around the camp so it'll burn to the center. As soon as the circle is complete, with a firebreak around it, we'll go on. After we all scrub up we'll follow the brigade."

That was a long day. Shadows were slanting along the valleys before we'd cleaned up to his satisfaction and mounted our ponies to catch up with the brigade. Just as we came in sight of the encampment, we met a volley from a wooded ravine. In the skirmish that followed, we soon routed this *new* bunch of several hundred Indians, for they were not from the same tribes as those we'd fought the day before. These were riding ponies without spots or patches of color. Many of them were buckskin or brown. Someone said that they were Sans Arc Indians. Our howitzer served them the same way it did others. They soon raced away.

The shooting must have stirred up General Sully's staff. He came riding out with Colonel Thomas just after the skirmish was all over. After a few minute's discussion that

140

sounded as if it was our fault for being attacked, we were sent to form a skirmish line around the whole camp, without any chance to even eat supper. But by then it was no new event to miss supper.

Company B was on duty until nearly midnight, when we were relieved and went to bed. I scratched imaginary lice, fleas, bedbugs, and nits all night. The idea of crawling things on your back is more persistent than the little monsters themselves.

Next morning we moved down into less rugged country and joined the emigrant train on Heart River. The combined force immediately started on the march to the Yellowstone River where we were supposed to meet supply boats. We were headed far north of the trail usually followed in going to Idaho. This new one was rough and unmapped. A half-breed interpreter seemed to be the only guide.

When I went down to the commissary for rations I heard the quartermaster explaining to General Sully that we were down to about a week's rations of hard bread and cereal. We had plenty of meat — horsemeat from ponies shot in the battle. But those constant mistakes in bringing supplies and food had me worried.

In fact, all of the Minnesota Volunteers were in low spirits. We didn't have the confidence in General Sully that we'd had in General Sibley. Of course Sibley had his critics.[15] But one detail after another had gone wrong on this trip into the Bad Lands. There was almost no grass for the horses and mules. There was bad water. We'd marched long hours every day, with very little encouragement. Now we were in short supply of powder and canister for the howitzers. For that reason we had to use the six-pounders even when the howitzers would have been far more effective.

Some of the light wagons had broken down on the trip to the Knife River and had been left with the excuse, "We'll pick them up on the way back." Now we were going to go through the Bad Lands on a different route to get to the Yellowstone River.

141

General Sully still insisted on cutting a road for the emigrant train and on keeping it with us. That would slow us down to where we'd never overtake any Indians. And our Eighth Minnesota still seemed to draw most of the hard work, pulling wagons and corralling mules.

Captain Pettit tried to take a cheerful view of the matter. "We can get along on horsemeat, Sergeant. It's stringy and lean because those Indian ponies we butchered hadn't had enough to eat. But it's food. I'll eat horsemeat, if only he'll keep after the Sioux as long as we can keep 'em running."

"But the meat we have won't last much longer. We'll have to get the Indians into another battle so we can shoot more horses."

"Don't worry about that. They still think they have us licked. We won't have to hunt them. They'll hunt us."

"That's what I mean. Are we hunting them — or walking into some trap? I don't like this country. From what some of the scouts say, who have been here before, we're heading into the worst country in the West for getting anywhere. It's just a maze of ravines and ridges."

"It's good experience. We're learning more about hunting Indians all the time. Now the best way to bring them out into the open is to shoot their horses. When a horse falls you get a chance to shoot the Indian before he can run to cover."

"Your idea of having half the men hold their fire until they can see where the first volley hit has helped bring 'em down, but it isn't easy. Those Sioux sure can ride. All you can see is one heel hooked over the back of a horse and his head bobbing under the horse's neck."

"But they sure roll when you drop their horses."

I was always amazed at the difference between Captain Pettit in camp or on the march and when he was hunting Indians. They turned him into a bloody machine, as cruel and cunning as the Sioux he was hunting. In camp he was always looking out for his men, caring for his horse, or showing the best of his cheerful and encouraging manner.

142

For the next two weeks we never knew what was coming next. We were on half-rations, except for horsemeat. We cut our way between hills of clay, then we filled in gullies and pulled down boulders. The only time the Eighth Regiment was in the lead of the line of march was when we did the pick and shovel work building a road for the wagons. If we followed a ravine heading for the Little Missouri, it would get too rough and we'd have to cut the road up along the ridge and cross to another gully. By the time we got to the Little Missouri our horses were more than half-starved. The best of the wagons were falling apart.

By now it was plain that the Indians were hunting us. We were no longer a "punitive expedition." The road we cut kept passing side ravines, where the Indians continually attacked in sudden, screaming rushes from the brush. We lost several mules and horses. By a miracle we lost almost no men.

At Captain Jones' suggestion we got permission to emplace a six-pounder in the mouth of each ravine as the head of the line reached it, and it would stay there until the wagons had gone past. With Pope's guns we could handle each ravine for several miles. It meant watching a ravine and defending our lines against a few or several hundred savages, then trotting past the supply wagons, the emigrant train, and our military columns to the head of the line of march and defending the next ravine we came to. But it payed off. Our brigade never lost a man on that part of the campaign.

The wagons had to go in single file for much of the march to the Yellowstone River. Since we were ordered to close up, we had to eat more dust. Many of the mules and horses were becoming humped with "heaves" from the dust. More than half of the drivers got sore eyes and had bad coughing spells. My life became a series of emplacing a field-piece in the mouth of a ravine, waiting for an Indian attack, firing a few (or many) rounds as they appeared, watching some infantry futilely chase the mounted Indians up a rough

143

ravine, then hurrying on ahead to the next unprotected ravine.

Meanwhile, the column and the slow ox teams of the emigrant train would slog past. At best the column was a mile long. In narrow places it was twice that. Musketry could be heard all up and down the line. Sometimes the Indians would wait on top of a cliff near the line of march and shoot down on us. We were under almost constant fire for most of the nine days that we spent wandering through the Bad Lands.

Crossing the Little Missouri River was only a minor hazard. The water level was low, but there was enough so that all the men could take a bath. Even some of the mules wallowed in the shallow water. On west of the river we found harder travel. It was all uphill until we got to the watershed of the Yellowstone River. And we had far more road to make. But we had fewer wagons and mules and less supplies to haul. The oxen and their heavier wagons continued to be just as slow and time-wasting.

But now the ravines seemed to be bigger. Pope's battery or Jones' had to shell the timber in each one. The number of Indians seemed to be increasing. There were more ceremonial exhibitions on the cliffs above us. And their yelling continued all night long. Some of our men couldn't sleep. I was tense, but too tired to stay awake. Guarding the train at the mouth of the ravines wore me out. Sometimes we were shelling the deploying Indians for two hours at a time.

Then one morning we came to a place where a road had to be dug out of the bank of the river. Colonel Thomas was detailed to dig the road and to flank the wagons. Colonel Pattee, of the Seventh Iowa, was detailed to guard the road gang. Captain Jones was to emplace guns in the ravine. By noon the column had gone on so far ahead of the wagons that they were out of the fight when the Indians attacked. Jones' quick support in bringing back two more six-pounders drove back the Indians.

Then the savages massed a far greater force and attacked the long line of wagons, apparently thinking they could

144

cause a disorganized retreat and capture the one six-pounder in sight. Again Captain Jones anticipated their move, brought back his guns and rained spherical-case shells on the massed Indians. My six-pounder with the rear guard fired canister at point blank range until the barrel grew too hot to touch. We used all of the water in our canteens to wet the sponge for wiping out the gun before reloading, but it was so hot I expected a misfire at any moment as I rammed home the powder bag and canister myself.

For more than an hour there was the rattle of muskets and rifles up the line of march. Captain Pettit rode back and ordered some of Company B on ahead to a needed spot. The rest of us held the rear until the last of the ox teams snailed by.

Then we were also climbing up to the top of a gully onto a rolling plateau. About two hours before sunset we came in sight of a small lake. Many of our Minnesota wagons were already camped around it. Captain Pettit rode forward for orders and came back to tell us that a big band of Indians had put up a stiff battle to keep us away from the lake and the spring near it. Again it had been our Eighth Minnesota brigade that had taken the brunt of clearing out the Indians. For awhile it had been touch and go. One of Colonel McLaren's companies had been completely surrounded by a horde of savages. By steady firing they had held them off until Colonel Thomas could send two more companies to their aid. The other troops had been busy setting up their own camps.

Report of Brig. Gen. Alfred Sully, Commanding;[16]

HEADQUARTERS NORTHWESTERN INDIAN EXPEDITION, CAMP ON HEART RIVER,

Dakota Terr., July 31, 1864,

SIR: I have the honor to make the following report of my operations since July 25th:

On the 23rd of this month I reached this point, having made rapid marches, considering I had a very large emigrant train under my charge. I had started in a direction west, but on the road, receiving information that the Indians were on or near the Knife river, I changed my course in a northerly direction. On my arrival at this point I corralled all my wagons and the emigrant train, leaving it under the charge of Capt. Tripp, Dakota cavalry, with a sufficient force to guard against danger, intending to start with pack-mules, but on opening the boxes found no saddle blankets. This I replaced with gunny sacks. I then found the bands that go over the packs and under the belly (called cintuas, I believe) instead of being made of webbing or several thicknesses of duck sewed together, and about six or eight inches wide, were made of hard leather about three inches wide. The torture to the mules, when these pieces of what ought to be called sheet-iron were brought tight into their bellies, was such that they were kicking and jumping in all directions and succeeded in either getting their packs off or breaking the saddle. I therefore had to give up the pack-mule system, for two days' march with such instruments of torture would completely use up all my animals. I then pressed into service all the light private wagons with me, placing in each four of my best mules and hauling 1,000 pounds each. By throwing away all tents, everything but provisions and ammunition, I could move rapidly with a very few wagons. About 3 P.M. of the 26th I succeeded in getting off, and about 10 A.M. of the 28th succeeded in reaching the enemy's camp about eighty miles march. All their camp was standing when I reached there, and they prepared for a fight, no doubt with full confidence of whipping me, for they had twenty-four hours notice of my advance, by a party of my scouts falling in with a party of theirs not sixteen miles from here. We followed their trail, which led me to the camp. I found the Indians strongly posted on the sides of Tahkahokuty Mountain, which is a small chain of very high hills, filled with ravines, thickly timbered and well watered, situated on a branch of the Little Missouri, Gros Ventres, latitude

146

47°15′, as laid down on the government map.

The prairie in front of the camp is very rolling, and on the left as we approached, high hills. On the top and sides of these hills and on my right, at the base of the mountains, also on the hillocks in front of the prairie, the Indians were posted; there were over 1,600 lodges, at least 5,000 or 6,000 warriors composed of the Unkpapas, Sans Arcs, Blackfeet, Minneconjous, Yanktonais, and Santee Sioux. My force consisted of about . . . 2,200 men.

Finding it impossible to charge, owing to the country being intersected by deep ravines filled with timber, I dismounted and deployed six companies of the Sixth Iowa on the right and three companies of the Seventh Iowa, and on the left six companies of the Eighth Minnesota Infantry; placed Pope's battery in the centre, supported by two companies of cavalry; the Second Cavalry on the left, drawn up by squadrons, Brackett's Minnesota Battalion on the right on the same order, Jones' battery and four companies of cavalry as reserve. The few wagons I had closed up, and rear guard, composed of three companies followed. In this order we advanced, driving in the Indians until we reached the plain between the hills and the mountains. Here large bodies of Indians flanked me. The Second Cavalry drove from the left. A very large body of Indians collected on my right for a charge. I directed Brackett to charge them. This he did gallantly, driving them in a circle of about three miles to the base of the mountains, and beyond my line of skirmishers, killing many of them. The Indians seeing his position, collected in large numbers on him, but he repelled them, assisted by some well-directed shots from Jones' battery. About this time a large body of Indians, who we ascertained afterward had been out hunting for me, came up on my rear. I brought a piece of Jones' battery to the rear, and with the rear guard dispersed them. The Indians, seeing that the day would not be favorable to them, had commenced taking down their lodges and sending back their families. I swung the left of

147

my line round to the right and closed on them, sending Pope with his guns and the Dakota cavalry (two companies) forward. The artillery fire soon drove them out of their strong position in the ravines, and Jones' battery, with Brackett's battalion moving up on the right, soon put them to flight, the whole of my line advancing at the same time. By sunset no Indians were on the ground. A body, however, appeared on top of the mountain over which they had retreated. I sent Major Camp, Eighth Minnesota, with four companies of the Eighth Minnesota, forward. They ascended to the top of the hill, putting the Indians to flight and killing several. The total number killed, judging from what we saw, was from 100 to 150. I saw them during the fight carry off a great many dead and wounded. The very strong position they held and the advantages they had to retreat over a broken country prevented me from killing more. We slept on the battle ground that night.

The next morning before daylight we started to go round the mountain, as I could not get up it with wagons and artillery in its front. After six miles march, I came in sight of the trail on the other side of the mountain, but could not get to it. One sight of the country convinced me there was no use in trying to follow up the Indians as far as I could see with my glass (some thirty miles) the country was cut up in all directions by deep ravines, sometimes near 100 feet deep filled with timber, the banks almost perpendicular. I therefore thought the best thing to do was to destroy their camp. This I did, ordering Colonel McLaren, Second Cavalry, on that duty. I enclose you a report of property destroyed by him. That afternoon a large body of Indians came onto my pickets and killed two. A command was immediately sent after them but they fled in all directions. They made no further demonstrations on my march to this point, which I reached yesterday, my animals well tired out, having made a march of

148

over 165 miles in six days, one day being occupied in the fight.

The officers and men of my command behaved well. . . . I inclose you a list of killed (five) and wounded (ten), and reports of different commanders.[17]

With much respect, your obedient servent,

ALF. SULLY, Brigadier General

HEADQUARTERS NORTHWESTERN INDIAN EXPEDITION CAMP OF THE YELLOWSTONE RIVER, DAKOTA TERRITORY, August 13, 1864.[18]

SIR: I have the honor to make the following report of my operations since I made my last report, on the 31st of July, on my return to Heart river, after my fight:

I assembled together all the Indians and half-breed guides I had to consult about my course. I had not quite six day's full rations on hand, and I must strike the Yellowstone by the most direct route at the Braseau house, where I had ordered two small steamers to meet me the first part of August. They all told me it was impossible for wagons to get through the country near the Little Missouri, without they went south, the route I started on before I was turned north by the report of the Indians on the Knife river. I would thus strike the Yellowstone, near the Powder river, and it would take me two or three weeks, and then, besides, I could not meet my boats there. One Indian, however, a Yanktonian, told me that he had frequently been across that country on war parties, and he thought he could take the wagons through by digging some through the hills. I placed myself under his guidance, and he took me in a westerly direction for three days along the Heart river; plenty of good grass and water, but timber scarce; the country filled with extensive beds of coal, in some places veins ten feet

149

thick. From what I have seen, coal, I feel sure, can be found in all this country, from the Missouri west to the Yellowstone. On the 5th day of August we came in sight of the Bad Lands, which extend along the Little Missouri, the valley being about twenty miles across; through the middle of this valley runs the river. When I came in sight of this country from the top of the tableland we were marching on, I became alarmed, and almost despaired of ever being able to cross it, and should have been tempted, had I rations enough, to turn back, but, on close examination of my rations, I found I had only rations for six days longer, by some mistake of my commissary, I suppose for he is not with me to explain, as I left him back at Fort Rice. I therefore had to reduce the bread ration one-third, all other stores, except meat, one-half, so as to make it last to the river. We camped that night with little or no grass, and but a few holes of muddy water. I have not sufficient power of language to describe the country in front of us. It was grand, dismal, and majestic. You can imagine a basin, 600 feet deep and twenty-five miles in diameter, filled with cones and oven-shaped knolls of all sizes, from twenty feet to several hundred feet high, sometimes by themselves, sometimes piled up into large heaps on top of one another, in all conceivable shapes and confusion. Most of these hills were of gray clay, but many are of a light brick color, of burnt clay; little or no vegetation. Some of the sides of the hills, however, were covered with a few scrub cedars. Viewed in the distance at sunset, it looked exactly like the ruins of an ancient city. My Indian guide appeared to be confident of success, and trusting in him, I started next morning, and by dint of hard digging, succeeded by night in reaching the banks of the Little Missouri, about twelve miles. I regret very much some gentlemen well acquainted with geology and mineralogy did not accompany the expedition, for we marched through most wonderful and interesting country. It was covered with pieces of petrified stumps of trees, the remnants of a great forest. In

150

some cases these were sixteen to eighteen feet in diameter. Large quantities of iron ore, lava, and impressions in the rocks of leaves of a size and shape not known to any of us. The banks of the Little Missouri are thickly timbered with cottonwood, and the river resembles the Missouri, on a small scale. We had now reached the river and the middle of the Bad Lands. Having dug our way down to this point it was now necessary to dig our way out. I therefore ordered a working party, with four companies of cavalry, under the charge of Lieutenant Colonel Pattee, Seventh Iowa Cavalry. I remained in camp to allow the animals to rest and pick up what grass could be found around, there being but little to be found. Some few of the men, however, without orders, took their horses into the timber beyond the pickets, leaving their saddles and arms in camp. A small party of Indians succeeded in getting a few away, but three or four of the men having some courage mounted their horses bareback and gave chase, causing the Indians to drop all the horses, which were retaken, save one or two. A company was soon in pursuit, but the Indians escaped through some of the numerous ravines and forests. As we saddled and hitched up everything at the first alarm, I broke camp and moved up the river three miles in the direction of our route, where the grass was said to be better. By evening the working party under Colonel Pattee returned, having cut three miles of road. A part of the company, however, by accident had been left behind. They were surrounded by Indians and were near being cut off, but by a hasty retreat they succeeded in getting through the deep gorge, where the road was cut, the Indians firing at them from the tops of the hills. They pursued them to the river and showed themselves on the top of the high bluff opposite my camp, firing into my camp, but a few shells from Jones' battery soon scattered them, and with the exception of a little picket firing there was no more trouble that night. I now knew that I had come upon the Indians I had

151

fought about a week ago, and in the worst section of the country I could possibly wish to encounter an enemy.

My road led through a succession of mountain gorges, down deep ravines, with perpendicular bluffs, so narrow only one wagon could pass at a time, intersected with valleys, down which the Indians could dash onto any point of my train. Stretched out in a single line we would extend three or four miles. The large emigrant train I had were ox teams heavily loaded, and it was impossible to move them except at a snail's pace; I felt more apprehensive for their safety than for that of my command, for they had with them a large number of women and children. Therefore I took every precaution for their protection as well as for attacking. I distributed my command along the flanks of the train and a strong guard in the rear, with Captain Pope's four howitzers, with orders for companies to dismount and take the heights at dangerous points, remaining there until relieved by their next rear company. I sent three companies of the Second Brigade, who had the advance, ahead with the pioneer company, followed by Jones' battery. Colonel Thomas, with the rest of the Second Brigade, followed on the flanks of the wagons, while the First Brigade followed guarding the rest of the trains. I accompanied the advance brigade. I had given orders that at every point, where the nature of the ground would allow it, for the teams to double up and park as close as they could, so as to close the rear.

After marching about three miles we came onto the Indians strongly posted in front and on the flanks of a deep mountain pass. They were dislodged after some little trouble, the shells from Jones' battery doing good execution, and the advance with other troops pushed on, while the pioneer party made the road. The Indians attacked me on the flanks and rear at the same time, but on all occasions they were repulsed with a heavy loss by the troops nearby, and thus we advanced fighting, hunting a road and digging it out, till we reached a small lake and spring about ten miles from our starting point, repulsing the Indians at every point with great slaughter. I speak partly from what I saw, for in their hasty retreat they had to leave in many instances their dead on the ground; they carried them off whenever they could. At the spring there was for a short time quite a brisk little skirmish, the Indians trying to keep us from the only water we had that day, and the day was so hot that animals were suffering greatly, having not had much to eat for two days. Part of Colonel McLaren's Second Minnesota had most of the work here. One of his companies in advance got separated from the rest and surrounded; they, however, got into a hollow and defended themselves until relieved by other companies sent out from Colonel Thomas' command. Their loss, however, was slight in comparison with their danger. Unfortunately this day I lost the service of my guide; he was shot, having ventured too far in the advance. He was the only one who knew the country over which we were marching.

The next morning we moved forward. The Indians were in front of us appearing as if they intended to give us battle. Probably about 1,000 showed themselves. I pushed Major House, Sixth Iowa, with two companies, and Captain Tripp's Dakota cavalry and sent forward Major Brackett with one company of his battalion, and Pope's four howitzers, dismounting the rest of the Sixth Iowa, under Lieutenant Pollock, on the right and three companies of the Seventh Iowa, under Lieutenant Colonel Pattee, on the left to push out and clear our flanks, and moved forward with Jones' battery and the train, Colonel Thomas with his Minnesota brigade, taking care of the rear. We advanced without much trouble, with a little skirmishing in the front, and also an attack in the rear. The enemy were repulsed on all sides. It was evident in spite of their boasting all fighting was out of them. A few miles brought us to open country, and the last we saw of the Indians was a cloud of dust some six or eight miles off, running as fast as

153

they could. They were better mounted than we were. The men behaved well. There were many acts of individual bravery displayed. A great deal of ingenuity in many instances was shown by the men in trapping the Indians, who, afraid of our long rifles and artillery, kept themselves at a respectful distance. Parties would crawl out behind the hills while a small party mounted would dash onto the Indians, fire and retreat, drawing the Indians into the ambuscade, when they would succeed in emptying a few saddles and capturing a few ponies. It is impossible for me to give anything like a report of the number of Indians killed, the fighting extended over so great a distance, and was a succession of skirmishes. There was certainly over 100 killed. Other officers feel sure there was double or even treble that number. It is certain, however, that their loss was heavy. The same Indians I fought before was engaged, besides Cheyennes, Brules, Minneconjous, and others from the south. This I got from my own Indians, who, during the fight, conversed with them from behind the hills. They met me under every disadvantage on the strongest of positions and were entirely crushed and routed. If I had had anything to eat and was not encumbered with the wagon train, and if my animals had not been without food so many days, I might have overtaken them, for they fled in all directions.

I would here state that in crossing the Little Missouri I found the country covered with myriads of grasshoppers, who had eaten everything. My animals were almost starved. I found this state of things all the way to the Yellowstone, and I was obliged to abandon and shoot a number of animals on the road. After marching six miles this day, we came to the place where the Indians left about thirty hours before my arrival. From the size of their camp, or rather bivouac, for they had pitched no lodges, I should judge all the Indians in the country had assembled here. The space they occupied was over one mile long and half a mile wide, besides which we discovered camps all over the country, close by this spot.

154

I found the lodge trails turned to the southwest. We still continued our course west by north, and the next day crossed a heavy trail going northeast toward the same point where I first fought them. It was evidently not all the lodges that went that way. We continued our way across country to the Yellowstone, which we reached on the 12th of August, over a section of country I never wish to travel again; our animals were half dead with hunger; the grass entirely eaten off. I should judge it was never very good grass in the best of seasons. The water we had to drink the worst sort of alkali water; this told on the animals. Fortunately, we here met the two boats I ordered to get up the Yellowstone, if possible, and the first steamer that ever attempted to ascend this river. These boats were the *Chippewa Falls* and the *Alone,* small sternwheeler steamers, the former drawing only twelve inches light; they each had about fifty tons of freight; very little of it corn. The steamer *Island City,* having aboard nearly all my corn, struck a snag near Fort Union and sank. The steamers attempted to go above this point, but a rapid shoal rendered it impossible. It was also (lucky) for the boats that we arrived when we did, for the water is falling fast, and it will be impossible for them to go down the stream over rapids below without the help of our wagons. Having no grain to recuperate my animals I had to again change my plans.

I intended to again strike across the country northeast, in the hopes of reaching the Indians again, but without any grass for several days this could not be done. I therefore crossed the command over the river, fording it without much difficulty with my wagons. The building of the post on the Yellowstone this year I consider not practicable. The loss of one of my boats, the impossibility of getting boats this late up the river, and the want of grass prevented me from hauling stores several hundred miles up the river will show you the reasons. I shall follow down the Yellowstone to its mouth, cross the Missouri and down it to Berthold. I will by this means have

155

grass and a good road, though I increase my distance by over 100 miles. I have the honor to inclose you the reports of commanders in regard to the part they took in the different skirmishes.

With much respect, your obedient servant,

ALF. SULLY, Brigadier General.

TO: ASSISTANT ADJUTANT GENERAL

Department of the Northwest.

Our Retreat to the Yellowstone River

I am quite aware that General Sully reported our "routing the Sioux and putting them to flight." Actually, they had harassed us from the time we entered the Bad Lands. If it hadn't been for Captain Jones and his skill with canister, case shell, and round ball, very few of us would have lived through that march to the Little Missouri, up the bluffs to the plateau and down to the Yellowstone. I've read Sully's report. It sounds like he was all alone, fighting a great battle unassisted. We were all trying to save our lives, and that's a fact. Most of the orders he tells about were what he would have said if he'd had the idea. Sully said, "Kill those . . . " And Jones did.

On the morning after we got to the lake and spring (when Colonel McLaren's men had to fight six times their number of Indians) our rations were further reduced. Most of that day we kept up a running fight, but we were beginning to set up ambushes for the Sioux, letting them chase a small group of us and then blasting them with a volley from a full company of rifles. Besides emptying a good many saddles, we captured more than a dozen ponies that day. Suddenly, in the afternoon there were no more Indians. We pushed on up to the open plain, or plateau, and all we could see of the Indians was a cloud of dust to the southwest.

Presently, General Sully ordered the lines to spread out, probably so that he could get out of the dust of the Iowa cavalry in front of him. The Eighth Minnesota continued all that day to bring up the rear and push the emigrant train, by hand and shoulder, up the hills and across the gullies.

On August 12th we reached the Yellowstone River. Most wonderful of all, there were the two steamers, near us — not at the place they had been ordered to go to. A rapids had prevented that. Again, our meeting was by the genius of General Sully —as he has explained. But it is true that grasshoppers had laid bare the country. That is probably why the Indians left us in such a hurry. They knew grasshoppers. Even the leaves and bark of trees had been eaten. Ox teams were so thin they had points to hang a hat on. Every rib was a ridge.

Here the emigrant train was separated from us and sent west in the hope of finding grass. Rumors of a new gold strike in Montana hurried them on their way. Scouts reported that the trail of a large band of Indians had drifted back to the northeast toward the Knife River. Captain Pettit surmised that the Indians were more frightened of the grasshoppers than of us.

"We'd better get out of here fast, ourselves," Captain Jones urged. "One more day without food and we won't have any horses or mules to haul our artillery."

The steamboat crews were also urging haste. They'd had trouble with sandbars and shoal water all the way up from Fort Union on the Missouri. The steamer that sank when it hit a snag had been trying to avoid a rapids. All its grain had been lost but now we had plenty of water and that seemed to perk up the horses and mules. As we hurried down the Yellowstone we found more grass. Then we came to the Missouri.

Even with low water at the end of summer the Missouri is wide and treacherous. It was decided to load all our supplies onto the steamers to be carried across. Some of the stronger horses, pulling empty wagons, made the crossing. As they were about to start, Captain Pettit made a suggestion, "Rope the wagon box to the running gear or the box will float away and you'll lose it," he told the drivers. "Besides, some of the boxes are tight enough to float the gear and help the horses."

The steamers made several trips across the Missouri to carry supplies. General Sully detailed companies from the Minnesota brigade to cut dry wood for the steamers. And the only available wood along the river, cottonwood and willow, burned fast and with little heat. One whole day was taken up in the crossing. One wagon turned over and was smashed and a dozen horses were too weak to get ashore. Three drivers drowned.

Accidents still hounded our "punitive expedition." Near Fort Union a band of Crow Indians overtook us to complain that they had been attacked and chased by a large band of Sioux. It may have been that General Sully wanted to know what bands of Sioux were on our trail, or because we'd found scattered grass and our stock needed time to graze, but he sent a squadron of cavalry back with the Crows.

No evidence of Sioux, or any horse tracks, were found. But the trail of a large herd of buffaloes that had passed in the night was plain. And we had been without any meat except horsemeat for more than a week. Again, I wished that we'd had a few hunters like Frank Pierce with us. He was a good shot. And he was also observant. He *sensed* when game was nearby.

By now the dry coughs and feverish faces of men strug-

159

gling to breathe were all about us. Horses and mules humped with the heaves from dust and alkali. The heat and dryness were wearing down the hardiest of us. Captain Pettit had become so weak that he had difficulty in lifting his bedroll onto a wagon. Once a coughing spell caught him as he was about to get on his horse. When it passed and the order to march was given, he had to walk along beside his horse, too weak to mount the animal. His deep-sunk eyes were far too bright for health and his long nose wore the pinched look of death.

Only the hope of reaching Fort Rice and the anticipation of mail from home had kept many of the men on their feet and marching. Many of our men were walking beside their shambling horses, preferring to walk rather than to be pitched from a stumbling pony. If the Sioux had been watching us as we inched our way back to Fort Rice they would have had good reason to say that they had the best of us in 1864. We had killed several hundred warriors and had destroyed the winter supplies of many thousands of savages. Now it appeared to be doubtful whether many hundred of us would get back to Iowa and Minnesota before we died of lung fever, bad water and exhaustion.[19]

Heading for Minnesota and Home

Dear Wife:

I once more write to let you know that I am alive and well enough to do duty but somewhat weak yet. A Boat has just come in from up-river and we have to improve every opportunity of writing in order to get them carried. We have not had a mail for some time but look for one every day. The last letter I got from you was dated July 9th. I have written as often as (every) two weeks since I came here (July 18th). We have not heard from Sully's expedition. . . . Capt. Fisk with his party of emigrants got here last Friday from Minn. . . . The weather is very dry and the grass is drying up pretty fast . . . I expect you would like some venison but think of the Potatoes and onions and lots of other things that grow in the garden. But hold on, the

161

Public Works will stop sometime and I will be my own man again . . . Oh! yes the wolves are thick as hops, they come right into camp nights and growl at us. Give my love to all the friends.

From Frank

On the 8th of September we reached Fort Rice and wondered at the considerable work on the fortifications accomplished by our men left there, many of whom had been left behind as too weak to travel. Sully didn't appear to be satisfied as he went storming around the entrenchments. Part of his annoyance was to learn that Captain Fisk had come and gone on — and was in bad trouble about 200 miles west of us, but determined to go on through to Montana.[21] Capt. Fisk hadn't known where we were and had probably blundered into the Sioux bands after they had left us near the Yellowstone.

General Sully sent two squadrons of cavalry and two companies of Eighth Minnesota to the assistance of Fisk's party, with orders to bring them back. We surmised that there'd be fireworks when Fisk was hauled back and met the General. Since the Eighth Minnesota couldn't find more than a few score of horses fit to travel, our men had to go on foot. (Men would be easier to replace than horses, or so he thought.) Also, General Sully left a strong detachment at Fort Rice to continue the fortifications and to protect the wagons and supplies left there.

The rest of the Minnesota brigade was glad to head for home. It didn't seem far, only a bit more than three hundred miles to Fort Ridgley. After marching more than eleven hundred miles in far worse country in the past six weeks, this would be a pleasant trip. This time we went by way of a new post, Ft. Wardsworth. It was west of Big Stone Lake and there was plenty of timber and good water. We rested there for four days. Several of the men got pretty sick before we got there. Frank Pierce said he felt a lot better, but he was thin and his coughing spells left him too weak to ride his pony.

162

But there were others far sicker than Frank. Alkali water and the grinding trip to the Yellowstone River had worn down Captain Pettit's determination. He was too weak to leave his bed on the morning after we reached Fort Wardsworth. Frank came over to where I was polishing my fieldpiece.

"We're going to have to get some help for Captain Pettit," he told me. "It was your nursing that pulled me through last winter. He's choking to death."

For the next three days and nights we kept watch day and night. We only left him to draw supplies and perform our camp chores. Lieutenant Hollister, as senior officer, took charge of Company B. He helped us all he could. But our nursing wasn't enough. On the fourth afternoon we laid Captain Pettit to rest. Colonel Thomas made a heartfelt talk about him as a scholar and a gentleman. Sergeant Pierce asked that he be allowed to read a chapter from the Bible, one that held a special meaning for Captain Pettit and several of his friends from Sauk Centre. It is one I've always liked. More than a score of Company B men bowed their heads and blinked away tears as Frank read:[22]

"Remember now thy creator in the days of thy youth, while the evil days come not, nor the years draw nigh, when thou shalt say, I have no pleasure in them; while the sun, or the light, or the moon, or the stars, be not darkened, nor the clouds return after the rain; In the day when the keepers of the house shall tremble, and the strong men shall bow themselves, and the grinders cease because they are few, and those that look out of the windows be darkened . . . and fears shall be in the way, and the almond tree shall flourish, and the grasshopper shall be a burden, and desire shall fail; because man goeth to his long home, and the mourners go about the streets:
Or ever the silver cord be loosed, or the golden bowl be broken, or the pitcher be broken at the fountain, or the wheel broken at the cistern.

163

Then shall the dust return to earth as it was: and the spirit shall return unto God who gave it."

Since June we'd marched more than 1,500 miles, fought in two major battles with the Sioux, and had practically lived off the hunting we had time to do. Captain Pettit was the only man of his Company B not to return to Minnesota. Some of us were even healthier than when we had started out. Even Frank got to feeling better by the time we got back to Fort Ridgley. He said it was eating fresh vegetables — especially onions.

General Sibley and the top generals and politicians had a lot to say about the traders who were supplying the Sioux with rifles and ammunition. On the 1864 expedition we all kept our eyes open for spent cartridges, and Colonel Thomas turned over a sackful of shells to the General to support his claim against the traders.[23] Much of the evidence was against the British traders.

In November we had a week's leave and went down to Freeborn. We both enjoyed that. Carrie had bought a new dress with some of the money Frank had sent, so she was almost kindly. At least she was pleasant to me and agreeable to Frank — until he told her he'd decided to get out of the army and go to farming. Then she let him know in no uncertain terms that she didn't ever intend to live on a farm. Frank decided to re-enlist. It looked like the Great Rebellion was almost over. I had been promised a commission under Captain Jones at Fort Ridgley. Frank was still First Sergeant under Hollister, the new Captain of Company B.

I saw Frank several times during the winter. He looked to be in better health than I'd seeen him for months. For most of that winter he was working outside but sleeping in warm dry quarters. Evidently he had whipped his old weakness for colds and lung fever. In April I saw him again and, in addition to the good news that the war was over, we discussed the furlough due us. We planned to go down to Freeborn together. I was get-

164

ting frequent letters from Susan. Frank was worried again. He hardly ever heard from Carrie.

I had big plans for Susan and me. Now that I had my commission I could afford to get married. I wondered how Susan would like my new beard. I had let it grow and kept it trimmed like General Grant's — and like thousands of other beards. The men told me that I looked more like the General than most.

Frank was going to come down by way of Fort Ridgley with a detail guarding a wagon train and we could go to Fort Snelling and then home together. But the wagon train came without Frank. On his last return trip to Sauk Centre he came down with black measles (possibly smallpox; diagnosis of the two diseases was not really positive in the 1860's). Sergeant Edward Patterson, who took his place with the wagon detail, told me about it.

"I'd had black measles when I was a kid so I tried to help nurse Frank, but it was no good. His fever went higher and higher in spite of cold water and wet towels. On May 14th he took his last ride — with full honors, on an ammunition cart. All of his squad were marching behind him with arms reversed. I led his sorrel pony and his boots hung over the empty saddle. Most of us were weeping openly and unashamed. We'd lost a fine soldier and the best friend I ever had."

I went alone to Freeborn, with a heavy heart, dreading to see his family — or even Susan.

165

References and Notes

1 The history of the Sioux uprising in Minnesota in 1862 has been recorded by many officers and officials connected with its suppression — but only from the point of view of the officers. The letters of my great-grandfather, Franklin Pierce, to his wife and to his sister, Susan, give details of the campaign that he and Allen Morgan endured, but from the point of view of the enlisted men. Much of the other information used in this book came from my great-grandmother, Caroline Pierce.

Excerpts from Franklin Pierce's letters are used here as the introduction to several chapters. The contrasting reports and letters of officers and officials also used are from *OFFICIAL REPORTS AND CORRESPONDENCE, MINNESOTA IN THE CIVIL AND INDIAN WARS, 1861-1865*, The Board of Commissioners, The Pioneer Press Company, St. Paul, Minn., 1893. In this list of notes it is referred to as *OFFICIAL REPORTS*. Note 1 is from page 238.

2 *OFFICIAL REPORTS*, pp. 162-165.

3 *Ibid.*, pp. 167-170.

4 *Ibid.*, pp. 171-179.

5 *Ibid.*, pp. 183-186.

6 *Ibid.*, p. 187.

167

[7] *Ibid.,* p. 202.

[8] From a letter of Franklin Pierce to his sister, Susan.

[9] OFFICIAL REPORTS, pp. 188-191.

[10] *Ibid.,* pp. 205, 222. General Pope's problems in getting supplies and men, pp. 233-239.

[11] Letter from Franklin Pierce to his wife, Caroline.

[12] *OFFICIAL REPORTS,* pp. 289-290.

ST. PAUL, MINN., Nov. 11, 1862

His Excellency, ABRAHAM LINCOLN,

President of the United States:

Your dispatch of yesterday received, will comply with your wishes immediately. I desire to represent to you that the only distinction between the culprits is as to which of them murdered most people or violated most young girls. All of them are guilty of those things in more or less degree. The people of this state, most of whom had relations or connections thus barbarously murdered and brutally outraged are exasperated to the last degree, and if the guilty are not executed I think it will be nearly impossible to prevent the indiscriminate massacre of all the Indians — old men, women, and children. The soldiers guarding them are from this state and equally connected and equally incensed with the citizens. It is to be noted that these horrible outrages were not committed by wild Indians, whose excuse might be found in ignorance and barbarism, but by Indians who have for years been paid annuities by government, and who committed these horrible crimes upon people among whom they had lived for years in constant and intimate intercourse, at whose houses they had slept, and at whose tables they had been fed. There are 1,500 women and children and innocent old men prisoners, besides those condemned, and I fear that so soon as it is known that the criminals are not to be executed at once that there will be an indiscriminate massacre of the whole. . . . The poor women and young girls are distributed about among the towns bearing the marks of the terrible outrages committed upon them. . . . These things influence the public mind to a fearful degree, and your action has been awaited with repressed impatience. I do not suggest any procedure to you, but it is certain that the criminals condemned ought in every view to be at once executed without exception. The effect of letting them off from punishment will be exceedingly bad upon all other Indians upon the frontier, as they will attribute it to fear and not to mercy. I should be glad if you would advise me by telegraph of your decision, as the weather is growing very cold and immediate steps must be taken to put all in quarters.

JNO. POPE, Major General.

168

HEADQUARTERS DISTRICT OF MINNESOTA,

ST. PAUL, MINN., Dec. 6th, 1862

Brigadier General ELLIOTT, Commanding Department:

About 11 o'clock on the night of the 4th instant, the guard around the Indian prisoners at Camp Lincoln were assaulted by nearly 200 men, who attempted to reach the prisoners, with the avowed intention of murdering the condemned prisoners. Colonel Miller, commanding, warned previously of the design, surrounded the assailants and took them prisoner, but subsequently released them. Colonel Miller informs me that large numbers of citizens are assembling, and he fears a serious collision. I have authorized him to declare martial law, if necessary, and to call to his assistance all the troops within his reach. He thinks it will require 1,000 true men to protect the prisoners against all organized popular outbreak. He will have nearly or quite that number, but it is doubtful if they can be relied on in the last resort. . . .

H. H. SIBLEY, Brigadier Gen. Commanding.

13 *Ibid.*, pp. 297-302.

14 Letter from Frank Pierce to his wife.

15 Oehler, C. M., *THE GREAT SIOUX UPRISING*, Oxford University Press, New York, 1959, pp. 133-140.

16 *OFFICIAL REPORTS*, pp.. 527-533.

17 *Ibid.*, pp. 313-315.

18 *Ibid.*

19 *Ibid.*, pp. 541-543.

20 Letter from Frank Pierce to his wife.

21 *OFFICIAL REPORTS*, p. 543.

To ASSISTANT ADJUTANT GENERAL,

Department of the Northwest,

FORT RICE, DAK. TER., Sept. 11, 1864

. . . I reached Fort Rice on the evening of the 8th instant. . . . I here learned that Captain Fisk and his emigrant train of 80 or 100 wagons (Idaho expedition) left here about two weeks ago on my trail to go to the Yellowstone; that he reached here under an escort of a company of cavalry. He required an escort from the commanding officer here — Colonel Dail, Thirtieth Wisconsin. The Colonel furnished him with an escort of a lieutenant and fifty men, composed of cavalrymen that

169

I left here, not in good health, and poorly mounted. The lieutenant with fourteen men returned the day before I arrived with a letter from Captain Fisk, stating that he was about 200 miles west of here (he had left my trail); he was corralled and fortified, and was surrounded by Indians, and that he must be reenforced to enable him to go forward, "for to turn back would be ruinous to him.". . . When my troops arrived next day I issued an order directing Colonel Dail, with 300 of the Thirtieth Wisconsin, 200 Eighth Minnesota, 100 Seventh Iowa Cavalry, all dismounted, and from the Second Minnesota Cavalry, Brackett's battalion, and Sixth Iowa Cavalry, 100 men each, mounted on the best of the horses, with two howitzers, to go after Captain Fisk and bring back his party. I would have sent a cavalry force, but this I could not; my animals were too weak to stand a rapid march, having marched 1,500 miles in the last three months, sometimes with little or no grass and the worst of alkali water. All day yesterday was consumed in crossing the troops and wagons, drawing rations, etc.; this morning early they started. . . .

With much respect, your obedient servant,

ALF. SULLY, Brigadier General

22 Ecclesiastes 12:1-7.

23 *OFFICIAL REPORTS*, p. 526.

Bibliography

In addition to *OFFICIAL REPORTS,* the following books were helpful and informative:

CENTURY MAGAZINE, Volume LXIII, No. 2 (December, 1901).

Chapel, Charles Edward. *GUNS OF THE OLD WEST.* New York: Coward-McCann, 1961.

Dick, Everett. *THE SOD HOUSE FRONTIER.* New York: D. Appleton-Century Co., 1937.

Flandrau, Judge Charles E. *THE HISTORY OF MINNESOTA.* St. Paul: E. W. Porter, 1900.

Kirk, T. H. *ILLUSTRATED HISTORY OF MINNESOTA.* St. Paul: D. D. Merrill, 1887.

Oehler, C. M. *THE GREAT SIOUX UPRISING.* New York: University Press, 1959.

171